THE FORGOTTEN

The Chinese Labour Corps and the Chinese Anzacs in the Great War

Dr Will Davies PhD (ANU)

With a Foreword by Dr Brendan Nelson AO and Preface by Albert Yue Ling Wong AM

WP

WP

Published by:
Wilkinson Publishing Pty Ltd
ACN 006 042 173
Level 4, 2 Collins St Melbourne, Victoria, Australia 3000
Ph: +61 3 9654 5446
www.wilkinsonpublishing.com.au

Reprinted May 2020

NATIONAL LIBRARY OF AUSTRALIA

A catalogue record for this book is available from the National Library of Australia

Planned date of publication: 04-2020
Title: THE FORGOTTEN — The Chinese Labour Corps and the Chinese Anzacs in the Great War

Cover artwork: Fang Lijun, '2016', 2016, woodblock print on silk, edition of 12, 244 x 366cm. Courtesy of Fang Lijun and Vermilion Art. vermilionart.com.au.
Anzac illustration by Ellen Naismith.

Chinese translation by Yan Qian 钱彦.

Printed and bound in Australia by Ligare Pty Ltd.

'Our reflections over the past four years on the service of the Anzacs in World War I have uncovered many stories. This story, tenaciously pursued by Albert Wong, and well captured by Will Davies, tells us of a contribution to the War, and particularly to the Anzacs, that few of us would be aware of. The Chinese Labour Corps helped sustain the Allied war effort, providing the manpower in the logistic effort to support the frontline. The story also reveals the feats of numerous Chinese who served in the Australian Imperial Force. It is a story of service with and support of the Anzacs worth telling, and is told most impressively in this book.'

His Excellency General The Honourable David Hurley AC DSC (Ret'd), Governor of New South Wales

'Will Davies has brought to fruition this book highlighting the "forgotten" Chinese and Chinese Australians who contributed to both The Great War and Second World War. We at the Museum of Chinese Australian History (The Chinese Museum) in Melbourne, see such a collaboration will hopefully bring to Australia an awareness of the Chinese from China and Chinese Australians to be remembered by current and future generations of Australians for their participation, sufferings and sacrifices in both wars. Lest we forget.'

Dr Edmond Chiu AM, Volunteer researcher, The Chinese Museum, Melbourne

'One of the great outcomes of our centenary commemorations has been the opportunity to tell stories of diversity and heroism that had previously been buried. Congratulations to Will Davies for digging a few of them up.'
David Elliott, Minister for Counter Terrorism, Minister for Corrections, Minister for Veterans Affairs in the NSW Parliament

'The forgotten ANZACs are an important part of world history, and vital reminder of the shared destiny of nations in the Asia Pacific. Albert Wong and Will Davies are to be commended for lifting this history out of obscurity, and animating it with the travails of long forgotten war heroes and the courageous feats of Chinese servicemen and women in many tightly fought campaigns. This vital research opens up fresh perspectives on China and Australia's common history, and rightly celebrates the shared efforts of these two nations to promote peace in our region across the last century.'
Andrew Forrest AO, Founder & Chairman of Fortescue Metals Group and Philanthropist

'This timely publication is a reminder of the contribution of the Chinese Anzacs to our efforts in the Great War as well as China's assistance to the Allies in that war. In so doing, it provides a reminder of the basis of the strong and

lengthy friendship between China, those who come from there and our nation.'
David Gonski AC, Chancellor of UNSW

'The Forgotten *provides an illuminating insight into the early relationship between a fledgling Australia and a China coming to grips with its place in a changing world. Australia has always been a nation of migrants, and early Chinese migration played a significant role in shaping our society. In these pages, Dr Will Davies shines a light on China's substantial but often overlooked, contribution to the Allied efforts during the Great War. This fascinating chapter in our history demonstrates how the Anzac legend touches all corners of our diverse, multicultural society. We must never forget the sacrifice we have made, shoulder to shoulder, in defence of Australian values which have built our free and prosperous nation.'*
Peter Dutton MP, Minister for Home Affairs, Minister for Immigration and Border Protection

'This book outlines the little-known efforts of 200,000 Chinese workers in supporting Allied troops during World War I and the exploits of Australian troops of Chinese descent during the war. I acknowledge this important work and the pivotal contributions of Will Davies and Albert Wong AM for their work on The Forgotten. *Thank you for sharing this*

story, which contributes to our rich and diverse history and will benefit future generations of Australians.'
Ray Williams MP, Minister for Disability Services, Minister for Multiculturalism in the NSW Parliament

'The Forgotten *is one of those special books that shines a powerful light on a little-known historical episode and in doing so reminds us of how little we know about important events in our past and thus of ourselves as a nation. Will Davies has written an eloquent account of the Chinese Labour Corps ('CLC') secretly recruited in China which supported the Allies, including the Chinese ANZACs, on the Western Front. In writing the history of* The Forgotten, *Davies has not only reminded us of the important contribution the CLC made to support the Chinese ANZACs on the frontlines but of the largely unrecognised contributions people of Chinese-ethnic origin have made to Australia more generally. It comes at an important time, when Australia is struggling to come to terms with the rapid rise of China as a major global power and the reality that people of Chinese background account for over 5 percent of the Australian population. They can now feel comfortably part of the ANAZC tradition. Albert Wong deserves high praise for supporting this project.'*
Geoff Raby, former Australian Ambassador to China 2007–2011

'The Forgotten *is a remarkable book published at an important time. This year* [2018] *marks the centenary of the end of World War I, as well as a time when the debate about PRC influence has taken a populist turn with the fingering of Australian citizens of Chinese heritage as suspected Chinese Communist Party conspirators.* The Forgotten *chronicles the largely uncelebrated contributions of Chinese Australians to our nation's sacrifice and heroism in the Great War, and thus our many of our national myths and legends. The book details the courage of many Chinese Australian ANZACs such as Billy Sing, Caleb and Sidney Shang and the Langtip brothers, as well as the unheralded role, airbrushed from history, played by the Chinese Labour Corps in supporting the Allied war effort in France and Britain, together with the hardship, racism, ostracisation and neglect they endured in the process. In doing so, this work reminds us that Australia and China have only ever fought side by side united against tyranny, that Chinese Australians have been amongst us building and defending our nation from the earliest days of non-aboriginal occupation, and that Chinese Australians have just as much a right to belong to this country and to be trusted as Australians, as anyone else.'*

Jason Yat-Sen Li, Senate Fellow, University of Sydney

'The Forgotten *is an important reminder that understanding our history is important to building the Australia of the future. General Monash himself wrote in his account of the war written shortly after its conclusion that it was the contribution of all that led to the great victories in France. This book reminds us of the importance of pulling together as a country in order to succeed.'*
Jillian Segal AO, Chairman, General Sir John Monash Scholarship Foundation

'Will Davies has brought together some wonderful material to give a salute to, and recognition of the Forgotten people from China who served during WWI in support of Australian troops. These Chinese citizens went to the battlefields of the First World War and worked tirelessly amongst allied forces to provide a number of services for the duration of the war. Many after the war stayed and formed the nucleus of the Chinese community in Paris. The way he has related the broad context of the war, the impact within Europe of course, and also the Chinese connection is timely. People should not forget the sacrifices that were made on behalf of freedom in that war and that the Chinese people, with their service and engagement, played a very pivotal part in an outcome for which the world is ever grateful.'
The Hon. Warwick Smith AO, Chairman, Advisory Board, Australian Capital Equity

'It is salutary to revisit aspects of history, even a History of the Anzacs and the Great World War which is so important to Australia and our sense of nationhood. But it is even more important to a minority group in our country such as the Chinese who suffered discrimination in the 1850s and who went on to prove their loyalty to their new land Australia when it was threatened as part of the British Empire by Germany and its allies. The Forgotten *is a story that needs to be told as we review migration in this land of immigrants.'*
John Yu, Australian of the Year, 1996

'They were victims of government-sanctioned racism. In the White Australia of the times they were outsiders. But they didn't hesitate to serve their country, both as Anzacs and members of the Chinese labour core. In short, they rallied to Australia. This is a message for today: Australian Chinese are good citizens and we must defend them from accusations of divided loyalty with sinister overtones of a White Australia.'
The Hon. Bob Carr, the longest serving Premier of New South Wales and former Foreign Minister of Australia

'Through an impressive and meticulous work, Dr Will Davies and Albert Wong sheds new light on a part of history. Beyond historical facts, this tribute to the Forgotten of the Great War reminds us the link between our Nations, united by some shared history.'

Nicolas Croizer, Consul-General of France in Sydney

'I am grateful to Albert Wong and Will Davies for making me and many others aware of this fascinating narrative on the valour and sacrifice of the Chinese Labour Corps in their support for the Anzacs and the Allied effort in the First World War. Will Davies sets the historical context for his compelling individual accounts of the heroism and suffering of many Chinese and their families. I hope as a result of Albert Wong's commission and Will Davies' scholarship, the Forgotten Anzacs will be forgotten no more and this book contributes to a more complete understanding of the complex, multicultural history of the major conflicts which shaped the modern world and our brilliantly diverse societies.'

Michael Ward, British Consul General, Sydney

CONTENTS

FOREWORD

Dr Brendan Nelson AO

Director of The Australian War Memorial

17 December 2012–23 December 2019

The Chinese Labour Corps comprised some 200,000 Chinese labourers who came from rural areas and worked under difficult and often dangerous conditions for the British and French on the Western Front during the First World War. As many as 20,000 of them died. Despite their service, most were deported in the aftermath of the war. Their story has often been overlooked.

For the Chinese authorities, the corps represented a way to contribute to the war effort without making a direct military commitment. For France and Britain, these men became an exploited workforce at the front, adding vital manpower to the collective allied war effort.

This book puts the story of the Chinese Labour Corps into the broader history of China's encounters with western European nations since the 1700s. A part of that story includes the large numbers of Chinese people who immigrated to Australia during the period. It was the sons, grandsons, and great-grandsons of these Chinese settlers who volunteered to fight for Australia during the First World War. Those men are the Chinese Anzacs.

The Roll of Honour at the Australian War Memorial lists the names of the more than 102,000 Australian men and women who have died as a result of their service in uniform. Among those names is that of Private Arthur William Moy, who served with the 39th Battalion in the First World War. He was born near Stawell in western Victoria, the son of Ah Moy, a Chinese man, and his English wife, Mary. Two of Arthur's brothers, Charlie and John, also enlisted in the Australian Imperial Force. All three participated in the major assault on Messines in Belgium in June 1917. Arthur was badly wounded in the fighting, and died of his wounds within a few hours. His brothers survived the war.

Arthur Moy was one of more than 200 Australians of Chinese descent who enlisted in the Australian Imperial Force during the First World War. More than 40 of them made the ultimate sacrifice for their adopted country, yet that country had not always welcomed their ancestors.

In the 19th century Australian colonies, Chinese people worked as miners, market gardeners, and merchants. Lowe Kong Meng was one such merchant, and one of colonial Victoria's wealthiest men. He had two sons who volunteered to fight for the country of their birth. The curious paths these brothers took are detailed later in this book. The elder served on the Western Front; the younger was twice rejected for not being of substantially European heritage. Men of Chinese descent seeking to enlist often faced this extra hurdle but, as this case suggests, the rules were not applied consistently.

Despite Chinese settlers being unwelcome in Australia during the 19th century, when war broke out between Britain and Germany in 1914 many Australians of Chinese ancestry rallied to defend their homeland. Some served right to the end of the war, only to lose their lives in the final weeks. Private Nelson Sing of Launceston was killed in action on 3 October 1918 near Montbrehain, in the Australian infantry's last battle of the war.

The Chinese Anzacs served alongside men of European, Aboriginal and other ethnic backgrounds. They too found acceptance in the ranks: among mates there was no discrimination.

People have been immigrating to Australia from China for two centuries, with the free settler Mak Sai Ying arriving in 1818. Since that time, Chinese Australians have participated in all of the nation's defining historical events. In some places during the 19th century they were subjected to racial and even physical abuse by European Australians, and to discriminatory legislation by lawmakers. Despite this, Australians of Chinese heritage have made a rich contribution to Australian history.

As part of the broad brushstrokes of modern history, the story of the Chinese Labour Corps and Chinese Anzacs honours their service. This book brings an important story to the public eye.

PREFACE

Albert Yue Ling Wong AM

For all those who gave it their all, for love of country and for love of those who come after us.

My inspiration for having Dr Will Davies write this book was a result of a chance meeting with him through our mutual friend and Australian rugby legend Nick Farr-Jones. Will had come across graves of Chinese labourers along the path on the Western Front, where he leads tours of the battlefields. He had spent some years seeking support and recognition for what he called 'the Forgotten', some 200,000 Chinese Labourers (CLC — Chinese Labour Corps) sent mainly from China's Shandong Province to assist the Allies behind the front lines digging trenches, laying rail lines and burying the fallen. It is believed that, by the end of the War, some 20,000 of these CLC perished from sickness, from starvation and as collateral damage. They were paid a pittance: many didn't have the wherewithal to make their way home. France kindly allowed to remain those few who became the genesis of the Chinese population in Europe. But the majority weren't allowed to stay. Even though they had helped to clean up after the War for several years following the signing of the Armistice in November 1918, eventually they were shipped home. They had buried the dead, carried the injured, removed unexploded munitions.

In our research, we also came across the little-known fact that in the Australian Imperial Force there were several hundred Chinese Diggers. These were Chinese Anzacs, in particular, the decorated Caleb Shang and the Gallipoli sniper Billy Sing. Of course, this is very much in the past, why bring it up now?

Like all things in life, I believe in timing and in fate. I did not go looking for this. It was Will who came to me; it was he who brought the plight of the CLC to my attention. I have lived in Australia for 43 years: it is my home; my roots are here. Yet until now, on each ANZAC Day, while I recognise a sacred day in our annual calendar, I have always felt like an outsider. I have not been able to bring myself to attend a memorial service, yet in my heart, I have always been grateful to those who made the ultimate sacrifice for Australia, to preserve and protect our heritage and values, our freedom and our way of life. I have wished to share in that sense of an Australian belonging. I am a staunch believer in preserving our values and our way of life; I do not wish to see the erosion of our

Australian values. We owe it to those who gave their lives to preserve our way of life.

My purpose in having this book written is twofold. It is, first, to recognise and to clarify the past. It is also to ensure that younger Australians and future generations in particular are aware of the Chinese participation in the Great War, that they know of the sacrifice made by Chinese and other ethnic groups including the Indian Labour Corps, Fijian Labour Corps, Egyptian Labour Corps and so on.

We are a multi-ethnic society with a diverse mix of rich cultures. We are also Australians; we owe it to ourselves to ensure that the Australian culture of fairness, inclusiveness and mateship is preserved and passed on. It is imperative that, whether they be Chinese or otherwise, new migrant groups embrace Australian culture and its values.

More than 5% of the Australian population is now of Chinese ethnicity; China is an important trading partner and friend of Australia. Like all good friendships, our two cultures may know differences and misunderstandings, but good friends should be able to see past differences and value what we share, both in our population mix and in our shared history.

It is my sincere hope that the friendship and the close bond between Australia and China, will continue to grow and strengthen. Perhaps one day, Australians will be as adept at speaking Mandarin as they are at using chopsticks.

INTRODUCTION

In my wanderings around the battlefields of the Western Front over a period of twenty years, I found the graves of men from the Chinese Labour Corp. They were often lost in the corner of a Commonwealth War Graves cemetery, removed from the other graves, often lined along the fence or bordering wall. They were rarely visited: they were forgotten.

I was inquisitive: who were they? I did some research. I found the story of their deployment and service. I wondered who knew of these men. Who cared about these forgotten Chinese labourers resting so far from their homes and families in far-off China?

These forgotten needed to be remembered. I initially sought a small donation (my guess was about $5,000) from the Sydney Chinese community, to erect a brass plaque, perhaps in Chinatown or, better still, within the walls of the Chinese Garden. But I could not secure interest or money. After four years, I gave up.

Then through my old mate Peter Tyree and Nick Farr Jones, I was introduced to Albert Wong. I told Albert the story of what I had come to call, 'the Forgotten'. Albert was immediately gripped by this unknown piece of history, as was his mother when he related the story to her that night. As Albert said, 'I went from being ignorant to being possessed'. This translated to his interest not only to place a memorial to these men, but also to commission me to write a book that was accessible to young Australians, in particular to young Australian Chinese and their immigrant parents.

This book is the result. In my research, particularly with the help of Dr Edmond Chiu and staff at the Chinese Museum in Melbourne, I also learnt of the Chinese Anzacs. This too became part of the broad story. My hope in this regard is to have Australian Chinese realise that they too were part of the Anzac tradition in Australia, that men of Chinese ancestry fought and died for their country. As Albert Wong said, 'I had never been to an Anzac Day dawn service or the Anzac Day march, but now I feel part of this tradition and part of this important remembrance occasion'.

I hope you enjoy this story. I hope that, like Albert, you will feel part of the Anzac tradition and its place in Australian society.

CHAPTER 1

TWO HUNDRED YEARS AGO

In 2018 Australia commemorated the arrival of the first official Chinese settler to this country, a seaman who jumped ship two hundred years ago, in 1818. Though some claim that the Chinese navigator Admiral Zheng visited Australia around 1421 with his fleet of huge, nine-masted junks of teak, 350 years before the arrival of Captain Cook, these claims remain unsubstantiated, even controversial.

But this Chinese settler was real. His name was Mak Sai Ying. He landed from the ship *Laurel* in Sydney as a free settler on 27 February 1818, just 30 years after the arrival of the First Fleet. Sydney was still a tough, hungry and remote settlement.

Life was especially difficult for the convicts, but for a Chinese seaman? With his limited English and Asian appearance, he would have been ostracised and treated as an outcast. But he came with skills that were in short supply: he was a carpenter and cabinet maker.

Mak Sai Ying had been born in Canton (Guangzhou) in 1798. He may have had contact with English traders and merchants in that important trading port. Like many Chinese who later arrived during the gold rush period, he would have had very little previous connection with the round-eyed Europeans with their blonde, red or sandy hair and fair skin.

Perhaps because of his skills, Mak Sai Ying found work with two of the large landed families. First he worked at the Newington estate of John Blaxland whom who he had met on the ship *Laurel* and with whom he had no doubt struck up a friendship. In fact, John Blaxland so respected Mak Sai Ying that he paid him the same wage as his free British employees, a most unusual occurrence at the time. John's brother, Gregory Blaxland, had been one of the first to cross the Blue Mountains in 1813. The Blaxlands were wealthy and respected members of society.

With his references and his woodworking skills, Mak Sai Ying also found work with the Macarthur family. They held extensive pastoral properties, especially around Parramatta and Camden.

After arriving, Mak Sai Ying anglicised his name to John Shying. In 1820, at Elizabeth Farm in Parramatta, he started work with two other Chinese: a cook and a house servant. John Macarthur found his Chinese workers reliable, hard-working and frugal, admirable qualities given his experience with recalcitrant convicts. Perhaps in these people, he thought, there might be a new and lucrative business, but he needed to get in early.

The idea of Chinese immigration was not new. When he presented his proposal for the establishment of a penal colony in New Holland, James Matra, who sailed with Captain Cook (and whose name lives on in what is now the Eastern Sydney suburb of Matraville), had suggested a programme of Chinese immigration to satisfy a potential shortage of skilled tradesmen. It would not be long before China, both as a potential market and as a supply of reliable, skilled labour, would find a place in the minds of the colony's administrators and landowners.

CHAPTER 2

A VERY LONG HISTORY

Long before the arrival of the Europeans, China was a powerful and very advanced nation, politically unified, heavily populated, educated, cultured and well capable of feeding its people. It was not, in European terms, an industrial nation, certainly not like the European nations of the Industrial Revolution, which at that time were leading the world in manufacturing methods, new products and advanced military technology.

The opening up of this mystic and ancient land for trade had long been a dream of European traders. While little was known of China before 1700, in the late 1200s, Marco Polo, a Venetian explorer, had crossed the country twice and written of his adventures. During the Age of Exploration, Western interest increased and countries including Holland, France, Spain, Portugal and Great Britain established trading ports in China.

Along with explorers and traders came Catholic missionaries, particularly Franciscans. They began in the 1300s, followed by Jesuits, who travelled widely across China, preaching and converting people to Christianity. While this caused great concern in the

Chinese Court and at times resulted in the banning of their teachings, others became confidants and advisors to the Emperors. Later, Christian missionaries became targets of violence. Churches were burnt and both missionaries and Chinese converts were murdered.

In the 1600s, more explorers and traders sought to understand and begin trade with China, but in most cases their incursions were restricted, and their trade confined to the coastal ports. The first significant incursion into China came with the establishment of a Portuguese trading port in Macau. In 1711 the British East India Company also established a trading post in Macau but Chinese resentment was building.

Recognising the relentless intrusion of the foreigners, the Qing Court attempted to restrict both the expansion of trade and the establishment of new foreign companies entering the market. Realising they were unable to contain this activity, in 1760 the Court introduced a trading system that came to be known as the 'Canton System'. This forced the foreign traders to deal only with approved Chinese merchants and not directly with the Chinese people, as had been the case.

By this means, China was able to maintain and contain Western trading influence into the early 1800s. The Canton System allowed the Chinese government not only to restrict trade, but also to limit it to just three ports: Canton, Macau and Hong Kong. Pressure from the European trading nations eventually forced the Qing Court to dilute the Canton System and in the late 1820s the new European steam ships were able to force the opening of ports and the extension of trade along the coast and into the Chinese interior.

From the middle of the 1700s in Britain, tea became the favourite drink of the population and the demand for imported tea rose rapidly. China was also a major export market; tea could be purchased in exchange for European luxuries including silver, gold and jewellery. Needing another trading product, the British began importing opium from India, an addictive narcotic which, while not new to the Chinese people, suddenly became available at low cost and in large quantities. While it had been illegal to smoke opium since 1729, thousands of 'opium dens' flourished where young men in particular congregated and fell into drug induced stupors. This naturally drew the attention of the Qing Court and efforts began to ban the import of opium and prohibit its use.

Events moved quickly. First the Chinese authorities blockaded the importation of opium in Canton; when the British demanded compensation, the Chinese refused. This lit the fuse between the Chinese authorities and the British importers who were actively supported by the British government. When a Qing official seized 20,000 cases of British opium — over 1,200 tonnes — and destroyed it, the British responded quickly, dispatching the Royal Navy to lay siege to the port. This action triggered what became known as the First Opium War. In a series of actions, they inflicted defeat after defeat upon the numerically superior Chinese navy and land forces, something later referred to in history as 'gunboat diplomacy'.

From this came the Treaty of Nanjing in 1842. This not only ceded five Chinese coastal ports including Hong Kong to the British but included a commitment for the Chinese to dismantle the Canton System and pay reparations to cover the cost of the war. In addition, the British insisted upon 'most favoured nation' status, ensuring their preference in trading matters over other European nations. All this was a major humiliation to Emperor Daoguang and the Qing Court, and a serious blow to China's national pride and international reputation, particularly as it further opened China to foreign trade.

For the Chinese, this was an unpalatable new lesson. They had not previously understood the huge disparity between the military might and technology of Britain's professional army and navy and their own primitive weaponry and tactics. The origins of this discrepancy went back 50 years to the inward-looking and unwise policy of Emperor Qianlong in the 1790s. This had its aftermath in the outbreak of insurrection and rebellion across the country as regional warlords took control from the central government.

CHAPTER 3

THE AWFUL CONUNDRUM

China was now faced with the serious dilemma of defending traditional beliefs or accepting Western ideas of reform. The disastrous First Opium War not only initiated rebellion and discontent among the Chinese populace but also forced the Qing Court to confront the intrusion of foreign nationals. Their new administrative ways, their technology and military hardware and their radical political reforms, certainly in Chinese terms, dragged China into the 19th century and a new future. While the Chinese hated the foreign barbarians, attention now turned to internal reactions to their reforms and concessions, which led to further rebellion and decay. China realised it must wake up to some unpalatable changes: a daunting and very painful prospect.

As if this were not enough, two other factors put further pressure on the Chinese government and the Emperor's now fragile control. First, there was a rapid increase in the Chinese population. Even with the introduction of new American crops and seed lines, food became a crucial issue which put strain on the Qing Dynasty. Second, widespread flooding compounded the problem and was blamed on the government's inattention to maintaining flood mitigation safe guards. In the countryside, farmers faced crop destruction and food shortages, and at the same time saw an increase in taxes and rent for their lands. Many deserted their landlords and took up arms against what they saw as a corrupt and vile system.

This turmoil brought on the disastrous and bloody Taiping Rebellion, which started in 1850. There began a period of widespread fighting and civilian chaos, reflecting China's struggle between the new nationalist, political and religious movements on one side, and on the other the traditional Qing Dynasty's power and control. Vast armies on both sides clashed. Casualties were enormous and those captured on either side were usually executed; villages in war-torn areas were plundered and burnt and civilians were put to the sword.

The Taiping Rebellion originated in the area around Guangdong. When the city was taken, it is believed that as many as one million people were killed. This was total war: civilians and animals were exterminated, farms burnt and agricultural land destroyed. During the 14 years of fighting, the rebellion spread across large sections of China and was finally quelled only with the assistance of foreign military aid and leadership. It is estimated that by the end of the rebellion in 1864 between 25 and 30 million people had been killed, more than the entire military and civilian casualties of the First World War.

This devastating rebellion forced huge changes on traditional China and on the power of the Emperor. Now China was 'cut up like a melon' among the European trading nations. Within China, urgent new dialogue began on how to address the many and diverse challenges; in particular, what reforms needed to be considered and introduced. This alone created a new tension within Chinese society, between those calling for radical change and a rejection of the traditional way, and those conservatives who defended traditional values, culture and the rule of the Emperor.

In 1856 the country found itself again fighting the British and the French in the Second Opium War, or the Arrow War. From the end of the First Opium War, European powers had forced upon China the expansion of their markets and undertook forays into the interior in search of further trade opportunities as well as the opening of new trading ports. Not content, the foreigners demanded more access to ports and trade, the legalisation of opium and the opening up of the interior. They also demanded that a British Ambassador be allowed to establish an embassy in Beijing.

The trigger for the war was the seizure of the British ship the *Arrow* in October 1854 on suspicion of being a pirate vessel. Though it had once been used by pirates, it was now a legitimate trading vessel. The ship was boarded by Chinese marines and the Union Jack pulled down. This prompted the British Consul in Canton to complain to the Imperial Viceroy, demanding an apology and the release of the *Arrow*'s crew. The British then bombarded coastal forts.

Soon after, French missionary Auguste Chapdelaine was executed by the Chinese. This brought France in on Britain's side. Amassing a large military force in Hong Kong, Britain began a series of battles with the Chinese, sinking fleets of junks and again forcing a treaty upon the Chinese Qing Dynasty. The British and French forces also looted and burned the Old Summer Palace after an allied peace delegation had been captured and tortured.

The Chinese initially refused to ratify the Treaty, known as the Convention of Beijing. This put further strain on the humiliated and defeated Chinese rulers. There was a demand from the European powers to establish diplomatic missions in the closed city of Peking (now Beijing). In addition, the Treaty opened Tianjin as a trade port, ceded Kowloon to the British, allowed freedom of religion, legalised opium and imposed a massive reparation payment to Britain and France.

Even though they outnumbered the foreign forces by ten to one, the Chinese armies were again defeated. The young Emperor Xianfeng was dead, the palaces were plundered and burnt and the once powerful Qing Dynasty was humbled and defeated. There was only one way forward: a concerted programme of reform, transformation and modernisation. This finally began after 1860 with the Self-Strengthening Movement. From this time a number of reforms were initiated, though often painfully, and in a limited way.

China was at the crossroads. Pro-traditionalists rejected Western influence and technology; anti-traditionalists rejected the old culture and ways; a middle group looked to adopt Western technology and, through qualified reform, wished to preserve the essentials of Chinese civilisation.

Where would China go from here?

CHAPTER 4

MEANWHILE IN AUSTRALIA

While this monumental history played out in China, and as the trading companies and European merchants grew rich, Mak Sai Ying was also improving his lot.

Having anglicised his name to John Shying, he married an English woman, Sarah Thompson. His hard work and enterprise enabled him to purchase land in Parramatta, and in 1829 he was granted a licence to run a public house, The Lion. Upon the death of his wife, he remarried, this time to Bridget Gillorley, again at St John's Anglican Church in Parramatta, one of the oldest churches in Australia.

At this time, the landed, wealthy families had access to large numbers of convict workers. They were virtual slaves as they served out their penal servitude. In many cases they were not ideal workers: they were lazy, unreliable and prone to escaping. The writing was on the wall for a continuing programme of convict transportation and these same families were looking both for new workers and for a new market to trade with.

Trade between the colony and China had begun as early as 1798. At this time, a boiling works was established on Cape Barren Island. Nearly 3,000 litres of seal oil was produced for China, and by 1808–09 sandalwood was also being exported into the port of Canton. This humble and obscure trading initiative was the forerunner of an important trading future for both China and Australia in the years to come.

China was seen as an ideal market place and the British were continuing to import opium as a trading commodity to replace silver. Not only did this have trade benefits for the British merchants in Chinese trading concessions, but it was also seen as a potentially lucrative source of income for wealthy, adventurous and resourceful entrepreneurs across the Empire. One of these was John Macarthur, whose business interest in this area had begun some years before.

Following the Rum Rebellion in Sydney in 1808 and the disgrace of Captain William Bligh, Macarthur and his friend Walter Davidson sailed for London, no doubt to face the music for their part in the Bligh uprising. Over the next few years, Macarthur and Davidson embarked on an ambitious opium importing business with assistance first from the East India Company and then from the famous trading house Barings. As far as we know, Macarthur himself did not travel to China. He kept a low profile in the business at this time, but it was probably through this association that he first came across Chinese workers and was able to offer them work and an assisted passage to Sydney.

The successful impression that industrious Chinese workers like Mak Sai Ying made on Macarthur and his colonial acquaintances no doubt pushed their thinking towards the future, to a time after convict transportation. By the early 1830s there were calls for the cessation of the transportation of convicts to Australia. This would alarm those like Macarthur, who had for so long benefitted from their labour and their service. Should transportation cease, who would replace this free source of labour? Certainly not English immigrants or even emancipated convicts. Perhaps, thought Macarthur, China could be a source of cheap, reliable labour: a business could be had in sourcing it.

And perhaps Mak Sai Ying, aka John Shying, could assist in this trade.

In fact, in 1831 after the birth of his fourth son, John Shying returned to China. Did he go with instructions from Macarthur to open trading opportunities or did he return for family reasons? We will never know. No one knows where he went or what he did and no records remain, but he returned to Sydney in late 1836–37, after the death of his wife.

With the end of convict transportation in 1840 there came new calls for an alternative source of cheap labour, particularly with the ongoing opening up of Chinese ports and access to the Chinese interior. For those anti-Manchu Chinese in southern China, here was an ideal way to escape the despotism and the social strife, and to find employment and a new life somewhere else.

Details of the numbers of Chinese who landed in Australia, possibly under the auspices of the Macarthur-Davidson trading arrangement, are not known. Sizable numbers seemed to have arrived in the 1840s, some years after John Macarthur's death. In October 1848, the ship Nimrod under Captain Henry Moore docked at Millers Point carrying 121 Chinese men from Xiamen, half of whom disembarked in Sydney. The remainder went on to Geelong. Between 1848 and 1851, nearly 1,000 Chinese men arrived into Port Jackson alone, and the following year, this number rose to 1,600.

Immediately, the community was divided. Some saw the Chinese as honourable and a potential replacement for convict labour; others saw them as exotic savages who would cause mayhem and social problems. Many colonists feared that with no women to act as stabilising influences and companionship for the men, the Chinese would be bound to commit acts of violence against women and create an unsafe society. Indeed, the roots of racism and fear of 'the yellow peril' had their origins in the earliest days of the colony.

When Mak Sai Ying arrived in 1818 Sydney, a struggling settlement clinging to the edge of the world, there was little time for racism and discrimination. Already the streets of old Sydney town were filled with faces from all over the world. Because Sydney was a port town, this diversity was obvious and everywhere. This acceptance would have been bolstered by good citizens of Chinese descent like Mak Sai Ying. Their community was hard-working, honest, clean and free of crime. They were in many ways ideal citizens.

However, events in China and, soon after, far across the Pacific, were going to dramatically affect Chinese migration to Australia. Within China, social turmoil and bloodshed were creating a growing wave of migration. People were keen to be clear of the rural dislocation, poverty, social unrest and the uncertainty of the future. This diaspora of Chinese people found expression in the goldfields of California from 1849, in Australia after 1851, and in the railway construction industry in Canada and the USA. Chinese people were on the move, looking for new opportunities, new wealth and a safer life.

The Californian gold rush started in January 1848. Gold was discovered at Sutter's Mill in Colomo, to the east of Sacramento, and in 1849, the first batch of 50 Chinese miners arrived. Soon there landed 300,000 people from across the USA and abroad, including 20,000 Chinese, all heading inland from San Francisco. The arrival of Chinese nationals continued until 1887, by which time there were over 150,000 in the USA of whom 116,000 were in California. Enthusiasm was helped by foreign ship owners publishing news of exciting finds, of fabulous new wealth and of the place in the world where gold was being discovered and fortunes made. This ensured they quickly filled ships with optimistic miners, their tools and possessions and also goods for trade.

Once in America, the Chinese offered the services and jobs vacated by those streaming to the goldfields. In the early days, the Chinese were welcomed. They provided labour, services and retail outlets; they worked as household servants, laundrymen, cooks, carpenters and shop assistants. They were seen as hard-working, honest, clean and unobtrusive, and although socially very different, were accepted as good future citizens and equal members of society. The Chinese welcomed the new world, the work opportunities, the food and the fact they had left behind starvation, war and social turmoil. Here too was a source of income that could be remitted to their families in China.

However, as they headed out to the goldfields, animosity and contempt quickly became apparent. American miners saw the Chinese as taking 'their' gold and working potentially gold-bearing deposits to which they felt entitled. This translated to harassment and violence, even death upon the peaceful, hard-working Chinese miners. Their camps were destroyed and their possessions stolen.

By 1850, just two years after the discovery of gold, the Californian legislature imposed a tax of $20 on all non-American miners. It was a large sum at the time. Then with the decline and crash of mining in 1853–54 and the subsequent failure of many businesses, the Chinese were blamed. Some moved to the new railway sites and became an important labour force for the construction of the railroads, spreading across the USA and Canada. Yet once unloosed, racism, segregation and violence continued. As late as the 1920s, legislation determined the fate of these industrious people, their ability to continue mining and their access to the USA.

In Australia, Chinese immigrants continued to arrive in small numbers during the late 1830s and

1840s. The flow of convicts from Britain was drying up and the need for labour became apparent. As they filled this shortfall, the Chinese soon became the third-largest ethnic group, after the British and the Germans.

It was the discovery of gold, first in New South Wales and then in Victoria, which triggered a major increase in Chinese arrivals to Australia. Soon the news spread across China along with stories of gold mountains and instant wealth. Once in Australia, the miners banded together in large groups and trudged to the goldfields, some taking with them saleable stores like picks and shovels, basic clothing, tents and the necessities of mining. Rather than focusing on gold only, they developed businesses: they provided the necessary services to mining communities in restaurants, retail stores and laundry services.

However, from the start the Chinese were made to feel unwelcome and their lives threatened. As was the case in the Californian goldfields, the Chinese were seen as 'stealing' the white man's gold, even though much of their work was re-working the tailings and the left-over spoil dumps from previous mining. Working in large groups and living in separate camps, the Chinese miners were ostracised and bullied from the start, not only by the miners, but by government and the official administration.

In Victoria, the site of the largest Chinese camps, numbers swelled from 2,000 to 20,000 in 1853. Riots and discontent spread. The Victorian government attempted to limit immigration by passing the first anti-Chinese legislation in 1855. This included a head tax of £10 on arrival. To avoid this, the Chinese instead landed in other Australian ports, such as Robe in South Australia, and walked to the Victorian goldfields. Seeing this legislation fail, the Victorian government next introduced a special licence on Chinese miners. This further increased tension and discrimination.

Based on the Victorian model, similar laws were enacted in South Australia and New South Wales. Chinese miners were refused naturalisation. Between 1860 and 1861, a number of serious riots — the Lambing Flat riots — broke out near Young in New South Wales, where an estimated 1,000 Chinese were injured, though none killed. But by 1867, as the gold rush was virtually over, anti-Chinese laws were being repealed. Most of the Chinese gold-seekers went back to China and the remaining Chinese were integrating into Australian society as hard-working, honest and good citizens.

The Chinese, however, were still drawn to Australia. They went first to Darwin after the town site was surveyed in 1869, when the population reached nearly 200 against just 600 Europeans. Two years later they went to the newly discovered goldfields at Pine Creek. New opportunities brought new immigrants, who changed the face and racial mix of northern Australia.

CHAPTER 5

CHINA IN A NEW WORLD

Meanwhile in China, the turmoil and instability continued. From 1861, through cunning subterfuge and crafty manipulation, Dowager Empress Cixi succeeded in consolidating her power and deflecting her enemies and conspirators. She installed her five-year-old son as Emperor and, with the support of the late Emperor Guangxu's younger brothers, executed three of the regents who questioned her power and control. After coming to power, her first job was to deal with the official examinations, a bureaucratic process every three years where officials from all over China came to report on progress over the previous period. By ensuring all officials over the level of provincial governor reported personally to her, she increased her power and control. To strengthen her control, she executed suspect governors; in the process, imposed an iron grip on power.

However, after the defeat of China in the Second Opium War, Empress Dowager Cixi realised it was time for change. The superior military technology of the European powers showed that a rural agricultural economy could not compete with one whose base was industrial and technological. Change was necessary. At this time, academics and forward-thinking officials began a series of reforms that included the construction of factories, machine shops, shipbuilding yards, cotton mills, a Steam Navigation Company to enhance exports, language schools, educational institutions and naval and military academies. They even sent young people abroad for experience and training in the hope of rejuvenating Chinese society through Western ways. But Confucian traditions remained deeply embedded, and these were largely seen as being at the root of China's problem in confronting the West, both militarily and economically, and in creating a new China.

In 1884, China was again involved in a war, this time with France. France had its eye on Indochina, modern-day Vietnam, and the Chinese were supporting the Vietnamese. In a peace treaty signed in June 1885, the French succeeded in securing the territories of Cochinchina, Annam and Tonkin, but the French failure in many engagements gave China new hope and a new military confidence. The French gave up Formosa (today's Taiwan) but they achieved most of their other territorial goals. Fortunately for China, the political costs to France dampened future plans for colonial conquest.

In China, this conflict further reduced the power of the Qing Dynasty and precipitated the re-emergence of a strong nationalist movement. As attempts were made to modernise and centralise military command, continual military defeats, particularly naval defeats, were humiliating. They dragged even further down the power and prestige of the Empress Dowager and the Qing Empire.

Apart from military defeat, Cixi still had to manage competing interests and the pressure for change. For example, the Qing Court believed railways were 'clever but useless' and Cixi banned their construction. This outdated thinking imposed hesitancy, indecision, diffidence and a lack of vision that stifled the decisive action that was much needed at the time. Instead, she continued her lavish spending, oblivious of the need for deep change, including the adoption of Western ways and thinking.

While European and American governments and traders had concentrated on opening up China, a similar situation was playing out in nearby Japan. Japan had not been seriously challenged until the coming of Commodore Perry's expeditions in 1853 and 1854. Unlike the Chinese, the Japanese were quick to see the potential of Western trade. In March 1854 Japan signed a treaty that opened the ports of Shimoda and Hakodate to American traders, allowed the establishment of an American diplomatic mission and provided for the care of shipwrecked American sailors.

Both China and Japan had a long history of isolationism and had closely restricted trade and Western penetration. China initially welcomed trade, but restricted it to select Chinese merchants in Canton, while the Japanese allowed trade only with the Dutch from the port of Dejima. However, by the time Commander Perry forced open the door to America in 1854, China had already endured pressure for trading concessions and trading ports leading to war. Japan was able to see how the European powers worked, what their military technology was capable of and what the opportunities offered.

As we have seen, China was slow to embrace an understanding of Western nations and culture. The people were inward looking and read only orthodox texts that were outdated and irrelevant. Their contact with foreigners was limited to the trading posts whereas the Japanese had actively studied Western ways, had even translated Western books, which in turn encouraged further study and discussion.

Japan embraced Western traders and technology. It quickly became an industrialised nation, bringing foreign technicians to teach and manage a new industrial infrastructure. With these changes came new administrative systems, financial mechanisms and coinage, taxation and political and economic management, all to the immediate benefit of the nation. Japan also introduced a constitution that gave legislative powers to an Imperial Diet. The work of reformers and futurist thinkers, part of the Meiji oligarchy, blended constitutional and absolute monarchy, in a model loosely based on the English and Prussian governments.

CHAPTER 6

FAR AWAY IN AUSTRALIA

These political, economic and social changes went unheralded and unknown in Australia. What is surprising, however, is that a trickle of trade began between Australia and China: the large wool broker Goldsborough, began to export wool to Shanghai in 1875. There soon followed shipments of pig lead, used at the time for the lining of tea chests. Refrigeration led to new export opportunities for food, particularly for frozen meat and fresh produce like apples, which opened new markets, including Japan. Issues of race and discrimination were forgotten: trade and commerce drove new relationships.

In June 1880, the aging John Shying is believed to have passed away. By this time he would have been relatively wealthy, and certainly well-connected to the Macarthur and Blaxland families. Given his contacts in both China and Australia, it seems likely that he was in some way part of this early import-export trade.

Like the USA, Australia was very slow to accept and assimilate the Chinese who had found a new home in the young nation. There remained a residual fear of the Chinese, their way of working and lifestyle, and

Australian racism dominated attitudes to the Chinese and deeply affected immigration policies. This attitude appears in the deliberations of a series of Australasian Intercolonial Conferences after 1863, at which the principles of Chinese immigration policy were drafted and agreed to by all states. These conferences were held against the backdrop of new gold discoveries in Queensland and Western Australia. Once again, restrictions were placed on Chinese immigration: Chinese miners were prevented by law from becoming naturalised.

This anti-Chinese sentiment continued. In May 1887 a large demonstration at the Sydney Town Hall demanded limits on Chinese immigration with few acceptable categories of entry. In 1888, the Chinese Restriction and Regulation Act became law, followed by similar legislation in other states. The fear of a massive influx of Chinese from the north was so strong in South Australia that a £10 tax was imposed on all Chinese who crossed an imaginary line 1000 miles south of Darwin. It was only Tasmania that had any compassion for the Chinese, allowing both the entry of Chinese families and a process of naturalisation, something ultimately prevented by the federal Naturalization Act (1903).

Yet there remains a substantial and little recognised legacy of Chinese enterprise, contribution and cultural offerings. The common Australian slang term *fair dinkum* comes from the Chinese words *din* and *kum* meaning true or real gold. This phrase is still used by Australians to describe as anything real, true, genuine or quintessentially Australian. So it would, perhaps come as a surprise to many Australians that its origin is Chinese.

Also surprising was that at this time an Australian journalist became an important figure in Chinese relations and the reporting of events in the volatile Chinese nation. In 1894, George Morrison, a medical graduate who studied at the Universities of Melbourne and Edinburgh and who worked as a correspondent for *The Times* of London, began his notable career as both a journalist and an advisor on Chinese matters. Over a twenty year period, he influenced the course of Chinese history.

During this time, Morrison reported on all the major events in China: the Hundred Days' Reform Movement led by the Guangxu Emperor, the Boxer Rebellion, the Russo-Japanese war of 1904–1905 that resulted in the defeat of the Russian fleet and the revolution of 1911 that led to the overthrow of the Qing dynasty. Later he became an advisor to President Yuan Shi-kai. Morrison attended the Versailles Peace Conference in 1919. He was devastated by the betrayal of China when Shandong Province was handed to Japan and not returned to China.

Morrison was also an early advocate of increasing trade relations with China. The Morrison Lecture, which is still delivered annually in Canberra, was established in 1932 by Chinese-Australians from Sydney and Melbourne to increase understanding of the culture, literature and arts of China, in the belief that better cultural understanding would lead to increased trade.

Morrison was followed much later by an equally amazing Australian, William Donald. He too was a journalist for *The Times* and other newspapers; he briefly advised the short-lived government of Sun Yat-sen in 1911–12. Donald was also a friend of Chiang Kai-shek and his wife (Soong May-ling), and an advisor to the nationalist leader Zhang Xueliang.

After the Japanese invasion of China in 1937, Donald ran an effective public relations campaign with Madame Chiang Kai-shek to help change the isolationist policy of the United States and gain support for China in its resistance of Japan. Regular reports from Madame Chiang Kai-shek were published around the world in *Life* Magazine, the *Boston Herald* and the *New York Times Magazine* as well as the *Daily Telegraph* in Sydney.

As the new century dawned, Australia became its own nation. A small Chinese population remained in the country, but residual fear and mistrust dominated Australian attitudes to immigration. The fear culminated in the infamous Immigration Restriction Act 1901, better known as the White Australia policy, passed in the first year of the new nation's parliament.

In its brief colonial history, Australia had seen great change, internal dissention, discovery and economical and political transformation. The interior had been explored and demystified, Aboriginal populations had been subdued and mineral wealth discovered and exploited. Boom, bust and drought had already established a cycle of life and death, and Australia too stepped gingerly into the new century.

CHAPTER 7

THE PROBLEM OF JAPAN

Unlike the Japanese, China's Qing Dynasty simply failed to understand that minor changes to traditional ways were not enough, nor that the West had also faced major social and economic dislocation with the Industrial Revolution that had created deep structural changes in traditional Western society. The Chinese saw Westerners as barbarians, while they, the Chinese, were the centre of culture and civilisation, again a very different attitude from that of the Japanese.

The control of Korea had long been a source of tension between China and Japan. From the 1870s, Japan had attempted to force Korea into opening up for trade, but Korea had been under the protection and influence of the Qing Dynasty. Japanese pressure soon opened further rifts, creating a crisis in 1882, resolved by the signing of a treaty between the two nations to share control and access to trade. Meanwhile, Japan was building a large, modern, European-supplied navy and an army based on European tactics and command structures. China was doing the opposite: reducing military spending and trusting in its traditional defences and an out-dated navy and army.

After ten years of haggling over control of Korea, war finally broke out in August 1894, after the occupation of Seoul by Japanese troops and a naval blockade around the Korean Peninsula. Fighting continued over the next eight months, and after a series of defeats, the Chinese signed a treaty with Japan ceding control of Korea, the island of Taiwan and other territories to Japan, plus agreeing to pay reparations. The treaty also allowed Japanese ships to trade up the Yangtze River (now the Chang Jiang) and to open trading ports and manufacturing plants. Again China was humbled, this time by an Asian neighbour rather than a European power. The loss of the Liaodong Peninsula also gave Japan a foothold in Manchuria, which became the starting point for the Japanese invasion of Manchuria in 1931.

With China on its knees, other European powers scrambled to claim their share of China through spheres of influence and trading concessions. This exacerbated Chinese fears of its take-over and subjugation by foreigners, which in turn led to further demands on the Qing Dynasty for reform.

Faced with a range of difficult choices, Empress Dowager Cixi supported the anti-foreign Boxers, also known as the Righteous and Harmonious Fists. They were a fanatical group who believed they possessed magical powers to deflect bullets. These radical groups had developed initially to rid China of Christian missionaries and to kill Chinese Christians, but further developed into anti-foreign forces, particularly after the late 1890s with the carve up of the Chinese 'melon'.

As might be expected, attacks on Christian missionaries drew the ire of European nations, who sent troops to protect churches, as well as their interests and legations. With an escalation of violence against foreigners and the arrival of an international force from eight nations, the Boxer Rebellion flared across much of eastern China. Between June and August 1900, the Boxers besieged the foreign legations in Beijing, but they were unable to drive the foreigners from China. Again, China faced defeat and a ruinous reparations bill imposed by the foreign powers.

At this time, Australia unexpectedly became involved with China through the Boxer Rebellion. It did not have a legation in Peking (Beijing), but on request from the British Admiralty, sent a force of 200 sailors, the 'Bluejackets', along with 50 soldiers from the NSW Light Infantry, and some naval ships. They sailed for Hong Kong in August 1900, but arrived too late to join the defence or liberation of the embassies. The force remained until April 1901, working in a support role, transporting supplies and men as part of the occupation force.

The defeat of China finally allowed the voices of reform and modernisation to be heard. It was the Boxer Rebellion that lit the fuse for a profound re-organisation of Chinese government and society that would continue for the next 50 years.

With the dawn of the 20th century, change, reforms and the beginning of the new, powerful China began to rise from the ashes.

CHAPTER 8

THE CLASH OF OLD AND NEW

Just as China suffered from the competing forces of tradition and modernisation, so too did Europe. Here the old ways were making way for the new, with the traditional land-based society giving way to industrialisation and the growth of cities. The old, established nobility now faced the industrialised *nouveau riche*, whose wealth came from mining, steel, banking, manufacturing and armaments. People moved in vast numbers from the countryside to the cities, driven off their land by enclosures or attracted to new jobs and opportunities. And as cities expanded, poverty increased. The trauma of widespread dislocation brought with it vast change, new socialist movements, unionism and large scale poverty and distress.

China, however, was in a far more dire and parlous state. By the end of the 19th century, China as a nation was defeated, humiliated and culturally dishonoured. While the Qing Dynasty lingered and the Empress Dowager Cixi still retained nominal control, China was already a very different nation from what it had been 50 years before. Forced by defeat to open up to the West, it remained divided and perplexed as to the way forward. It faced a conundrum: Chinese traditions versus the demands of modern reform.

While calls for reform were insistent and ubiquitous, change was still fiercely resisted by the ruling Qing Dynasty. Along with many in the Qing Court, Empress Dowager Cixi not only feared a loss of power, but also believed the greatness of China lay in their long-established control and their traditional past. In 1898, the young Emperor Guangxu saw the failure of his Hundred Day Reform, a brief attempt, under the influence of reformers, intellectuals and a cultural elite, to initiate changes. His reforms were rejected unequivocally by Dowager Empress Cixi and soon after, he was confined to house arrest on her orders and was to die a young man without any further involvement in Chinese history.

During the Boxer Rebellion, Dowager Cixi had fled Beijing to Xi'an (the start of the Silk Road and the site of the Terracotta Warriors Museum) dressed as a peasant. After yet another humiliating victory by the European armies, she returned to the capital. Although she actively supported the defeated Boxers, she escaped punishment.

Quickly, Cixi at last tried to implement limited reforms, but these were simply too little too late. A much bigger and important problem was the abolition of the 2,000-year-old Confusion examination system as mentioned above. She sent Court officials to Europe and Japan to understand foreign ways in preparation for the drafting of wide-ranging changes to Chinese society, government, the legal system, education and the administration. Ironically, many of these same reforms had been suggested to her in 1898 by those she had executed after the failure of the Hundred Day Reform movement.

The reform programme was varied and extensive. It improved the legal system, curtailed cruel and violent punishments, allowed the modernisation of the railways, reformed the currency, the national economy and government, and introduced reforms within the military with a new national army. Education was also improved with new Western style schools teaching Western subjects.

Cixi attempted to reach out to foreigners in residence in the capital, particularly the wives of the diplomatic corps. She held morning teas in the new Summer Palace, and even agreed to have her portrait painted by an American artist for exhibition in the St Louis World Fair of 1904. This was all part of the new China, but the emerging forces of revolution and changes were already beating at her door.

Close to death in mid-November 1908, the vindictive Cixi had one last mission: to eliminate the Emperor Guangxu who she feared might reverse her reforms and introduce, as he had tried to do in 1898, more radical changes within Chinese society and government. Given a massive dose of arsenic, he died on 14 November, the very day Cixi installed the two-year-old Puyi as the new Emperor. On the following day, 15 November, she also died.

With the death of Dowager Empress Cixi, the Qing Dynasty finally fell apart. During this time, prominent thinkers, reformers and political agitators began to espouse new political options, having decided the traditional Manchu imperial system was obsolete and that Western style democracy was a more appropriate system of government. From this came visions of a new China where traditional ideals were mixed with new ways or rejected entirely. This became the constant debate: how to modernise China and retain traditional cultural values and beliefs.

CHAPTER 9

A NEW DIRECTION FOR OLD CHINA

A major thinker and revolutionary at this time was Sun Yat-sen. Born into a poor rural family near Guangzhou, he was educated in missionary schools in Hong Kong and Hawaii. He then studied medicine and became a doctor, but soon turned to politics, influenced as he was by his membership of secret societies and his time abroad. In 1894, Sun formed the Revolutionary Alliance, composed of students and members of Chinese secret societies. The following year, as its leader, he helped organise the failed Canton uprising against the Emperor. After this, he went into exile, travelling widely for 16 years and not returning to China until 1911. By this time, dissidents had drafted a timetable for the introduction of democratic processes, to consist of a constitutional monarchy and a parliament.

With the death of Cixi and the power vacuum that resulted, the time was right for the overthrow of the Qing Dynasty and the creation of the new republic. Between 1908 and 1911, various revolutionary groups were formed all over the country, with aims ranging from limited change, to the complete overthrow of the ruling elite and the introduction of a republic. During these years, there were constant uprisings, revolts and riots against what remained of the Qing Court under Puyi.

The earliest anti-Qing groups had their origins outside China, often with ex-patriots, intellectuals and political dissidents like Sun Yet-sen who observed foreign ways and moulded their vision of a new China on their experiences. When they returned, they often had radically different views and ways to achieve democratic change. Some worked through changes to traditional values; others sought radical means through anarchy, terrorism, violence and assassination. From within these widely ranging groups would come the political and social leaders of the future.

The trigger for the final showdown came from a railway dispute in Wuchang in Hubei Province. The provincial government was unable to pay for construction so foreign loans were sought. This was greatly resented by the populace at large, and rioting began. As local resistance stiffened, the Qing Dynasty brought in troops to quell the riots, a hugely unpopular move, which led to greater resistance in the form of massive rallies and widespread strikes. After the leaders of the Railway Protection League were arrested and troops fired on the demonstrators, the crisis escalated as people joined the revolt, turning on the government and the local authorities.

Hearing from press reports of the success of the Wuchang uprising, Sun Yet-sen returned to China from America, arriving in late December 1911. He was elected Provisional President at a meeting in Nanking (Nanjing) and 1 January 1912 was nominated as the first day of the new Provisional Government of the Republic of China. In his inauguration speech he pledged 'to overthrow the despotic government led by the Qing, consolidate the Republic of China and plan for the welfare of the people'.

The Qing Dynasty was at this time still a force to be reckoned with. Without military forces to defeat the old regime, Sun Yet-sen was forced to negotiate with the commander of the Beiyang Army, General Yuan Shikai. The deal was to hand over the Presidency to him if he was able to persuade the Qing Emperor to abdicate, or failing that, force him from office. Yuan put pressure on the young Emperor Puyi who abdicated in return for a guarantee of safety for himself and his mother, the Empress Dowager Longyu. This he did on 12 February 1912.

Sun Yet-sen honoured his deal with General Yuan, who became Provisional President in February

1912 and was sworn in on 10 March the same year. So the brief period of relative calm under the Presidency of Sun Yet-sen was short-lived. Sun soon found that General Yuan ignored the republican ideals, and the provisional constitution that had been drawn up was all but forgotten. Instead, he ruled by tyranny and the power of the military, even dissolving the ruling organisation, the Kuomintang (Guomindang) and threatening the new senators with death. By 1915, Yuan had declared himself Emperor, but he stood down in the face of widespread resistance and the loss of his military support. He died the following year.

While China struggled to overcome the old regime and find a suitable, workable alternative among the many proposals, models and theories put forward, outside China tensions were growing. The race for colonies and trade concessions, while virtually over, had left a worldwide trail of colonial destruction and dislocation as profound as that in China. All this was set against similar social turmoil and upheaval in Europe.

CHAPTER 10

NEW TENSIONS FAR FROM CHINA

International tensions were challenging the old order everywhere. Just as the European race for trading ports had deeply affected the old Chinese Empire, these same European nations were reshaping nations across the world as they forced themselves upon non-industrialised, often tribal nations, taking control of their economies, wealth, resources and populations.

To service this trade and the demands of an empire, shipping was required and a navy to protect it. Now the great naval race began, particularly between Britain and Germany, to safeguard their trade routes and their life-lines of food and raw materials. This in turn required ports, hence the establishment of the treaty port of Tsingtao (Qingdao) in Shandong Province by the Germans.

This was a direct challenge to the British navy, particularly by Germany. The challenge created tensions. Nations now aligned, signed treaties and looked to re-arm. Fearing encirclement, Germany formed an alliance with Austria and Italy; the French formed an alliance with Russia and Britain. The tinder box of the Balkans, particularly the decaying Hapsburg Empire, also increased tension: Austria turned to Germany for support, the Slavic people of the Serbian Empire, part of the Hapsburg Empire, looked to Russia. The growing world crisis quickly moved out of the hands of statesmen and monarchs and into a revolving cycle of threat and counter-threat.

The world was on a collision course for war. China would not be spared.

As the Western powers drew closer to war in 1913 and early 1914, China realised it could be torn apart by the warring nations, having delegations, trading ports and concessions with Britain, France, Russia and America on one side and Germany on the other. These foreign powers also had their own alliances concerning China like the one between Britain and Japan which in turn involved France and Russia. While Germany remained clear of such alliances, Kiautschou (Jiaozhou) Bay was important as a trading centre and as a strategic port for the German navy, now patrolling in the Asia-Pacific area. These concessions were something the Chinese might regain if Germany lost the war. The USA was also involved, but prior to the declarations of war in July–August 1914, America remained removed and non-committal, pursuing her open-door trade policy and an isolationist approach to foreign policy.

The mix of internal social disorder, the forced change to traditional ways, the new industrialisation and the resulting poverty, saw Europe begin to split apart. Nations were divided and fearful, so they forced alliances. The crumbling Austrian Hapsburg Empire looked to Germany for support against its recalcitrant Slavic states in what is now Yugoslavia; the French, Russians and British formed their own alliances and treaties for mutual support.

By 1914, the world was spinning out of control, certainly out of the control of the kings and regents of Europe. With the assassination of Archduke Franz Ferdinand, the heir to the Austrian throne, the fuse was lit for what became the First World War. China could only stand back powerless. But so too could the nations of Europe: it was all too late. On 4 August 1914, after Germany had crossed the Belgian frontier on their invasion route into France, Britain declared war on Germany.

This broad context of warlike manoeuvring, strategic manipulation and threats, was played out in China against a confused and humiliating history over the preceding one hundred years. To understand China was to understand this recent turbulent past: the tension between the old and the new, the intrusion of foreigners, the wars and famines that caused vast loss of life, and the deep uncertainty for the future.

This history and turmoil were directly linked to foreign intervention. Now further dislocation, and the threat of a European war fought out on Chinese soil, was of great concern to the new Chinese leadership.

CHAPTER 11

THE HARD CHOICE

As the clouds of war approached and as the Europeans manoeuvred in China and the adjoining seas, China realised that it must quickly declare its neutrality. On 6 August 1914, two days after Britain declared war, the Chinese government proclaimed its neutrality and warned foreign nations about undertaking military operations anywhere in China. This proclamation said that this was a European war, a conflict between the same imperialist powers that had subjugated and destroyed traditional China and brought so much grief and humiliation.

The Japanese had no intention of respecting Chinese calls for neutrality. On 15 August, less than two weeks after the declaration of war, Japan demanded the Germans vacate the colony in Kiautschou by 15 September and followed this up with the declaration of war against Germany on 23 August. Japan thus became one of the Allied nations against Germany.

Soon afterwards and with Britain's help, Japan then blockaded Kiautschou. A few weeks later, Japan landed troops near Longkou from where they marched on the old German colony. By November, the Germans had surrendered and were taken into Japanese captivity, many until 1919. While the Chinese protested against this fighting, it was to constitute the only land warfare or act of war on Chinese soil during the whole of the First World War.

While China was fortunate not to be actively involved in the War, the war at sea in the Far East suddenly involved China. This went back to the mid-1890s when the Germans had formed the East Asia Squadron. This operated mainly in the Pacific Ocean and was an independent squadron, the only one not operating out of home ports in Germany. In 1897, the Germans seized and occupied Chinese built fortifications at Kiautschou. The following year they forced the Qing Dynasty to hand over an area comprising 552 square kilometres to Germany under what was known as the Kiautschou Bay concession. This was a 99-year lease for the area around Kiautschou which included the small fishing village of Tsingtao, with narrow, dirt streets and fragile, dilapidated housing.

The Germans immediately began a massive building programme. They constructed government buildings and European style housing; they provided electricity and fresh water. In the port area, the Germans built wharves and dockyards, warehouses and arsenals to provide facilities which became the home base for the Far East Squadron. Having this, the Germans were able to conduct operations throughout the Pacific, reassured they had a supply, re-coaling and repair base for their fleet.

Australia followed Britain with a declaration of war the following day. Immediately mobilisation began and the recruiting tables across the nation were thronged with excited volunteers. Australia quickly promised both a contingent of 20,000 men for service in Europe and an expeditionary force to sail for the German processions in German New Guinea to the north, where the long-distance radio stations linked the German home fleet to their bases in the east, particularly Tsingtao in China.

So it was that for the first half of 1914, the Germans carried out a series of cruises in both Chinese and Japanese waters. With the declaration of war, they immediately turned to aggressive operations. On 31 July 1914, the SMS *Emden* put to sea, and three days later and a day after the declaration of war with Russia, captured the Russian steamer *Ryazan* and sailed it back to Tsingtao.

After this incident, the *Emden* again sailed from Tsingtao. Over the next three months, it undertook an amazing voyage of destruction and the sinking and capture of two Entente warships and 16 steamers. In one audacious raid, the *Emden* sailed into Madras harbour where it destroyed fuel tanks and harbour installations. From there, sinking a number of vessels along the way, *Emden* made a surprise attack on Penang in British Malaya where it destroyed the Russian cruiser *Zhemchug* then undergoing repairs, and sank another French destroyer the *Mousquet* as it left port.

By now the *Emden* was a hunted ship and a long way from her home port in Tsingtao which had in the meantime been captured by the Japanese. *Emden*'s captain, Karl von Müller, then decided to capture the British radio station on Cocos Islands and at the same time, draw away British naval ships known to be searching for the *Emden* in the northern Indian Ocean.

His approach to the island was observed by the wireless station personnel who sent a signal: *'Unidentified ship off entrance'.* This was picked up by the Australian light cruiser HMAS *Sydney*, then escorting the first contingent of Australian troops to Egypt. The *Sydney* was about 50 nautical miles away (80 kilometres). It quickly turned north, and headed for the *Emden*'s location. After an unequal fight, the *Emden* was driven onto the Cocos Islands where it was destroyed by gunfire and the remaining crew captured. This ended all naval and military operations out of the Tsingtao port and freed China from the threat of further fighting on her shores.

With the rumblings of war in Europe, what now began to take shape in China was a change in the Chinese view of the world and of her place in it. A new nationalism and a new internationalism began to transcend even traditional views. It was fostered by an emerging anti-traditional view internally and the need to reach out and engage with the world and international affairs like never before. This international war, China realised, would have profound and long-lasting implications: it offered China new opportunities and allowed the nation to join the world order as an equal member.

So, for the Chinese, the next question was this: how to engage in this War and what might be the end results of such engagement. The general view was that the War would be over by Christmas, that either Germany would be quickly victorious in France and Russia, and that in the process, the British, the main offender over many years of Chinese aggression, would also be defeated.

Alternatively, the Allies, France, Britain and Russia, might be victorious. This would release China from the Kiautschou Bay concession. But in the short-term China realised, it must sit on its hands and stay clear of a war it had no part in and no influence over. Whoever won, China would be released from its concessions to the losing nations and gain a starting point for the building of a new post-war China along western, non-traditional lines.

With this long-term goal in mind, General Yuan approached the British minister to China, John Jordon. He offered 50,000 troops to join a combined operation to take back Tsingtao and to stall future Japanese ambitions in their territory. Jordon refused any such initiative, but again the Chinese asked Britain for help, particularly after Japan presented China in January 1915 with the 'Twenty One Demands'. These severe Japanese terms forced upon China the potential of further exploitation to the point of its becoming a vassal territory and a source of raw materials and produce. This naturally focused China's attention on both the War in the immediate future and on the peace conference far into the future. For China, the challenge was how it might win a place at the peace conference table and the best way to achieve this.

CHAPTER 12

TAKING SIDES

China now had to decide which side to support. The Allies seemed the likely winner but Japan, now her main enemy, was on the side of the Allies. The answer to this awful contradiction lay in China's desperate need for international status and recognition. A way must be found to engage in the War on one hand, but to retain its declared neutrality on the other. How was it to do this?

The voice of this new policy and creative thinking was a brilliant and influential politician, Liang Shiyi. Liang had come through the public service with particular experience in the railways which had provided both a deep, valuable understanding and powerful friends. He was a confidant to General Yuan. He was able to influence the General with his forward views on foreign policy and his belief that the European war would provide a great opportunity for the future China. Apart from recommending the end of reparation payments for the Boxer Rebellion and the restoration of the Shandong Province, he suggested options for the Chinese involvement in the War.

Realising China's need to join the War in some

form other than militarily, Liang Shiyi suggested a number of ways. His aims were to improve China's international reputation, to rid itself of its shameful past and to set up its future status. Realising he could not commit Chinese troops, he quickly came up with a plan based not on military aid but on labour. First, by sending manual labour, China could show support for the allied cause without violating her neutrality. Second, by contracting this labour through ostensibly 'private' companies, China could support the Allied war effort yet stand above accusations of contravening its declared neutrality.

Both the British and the French refused Chinese aid, even ignoring Liang's labour plan and offers of help. The bloody attrition on the Western Front and the severe shortage of men for the Allied armies reversed their view. Even by the end of 1914, after the French had barely saved Paris with their casualties already numbering 300,000, and as the opposing front lines started their long stagnant war, help from another quarter was badly needed. Now Liang's proposals had merit and the basic idea of a Chinese labour contingent formed in the minds of the Allies, in particular the French.

For the Chinese, this was an honourable, deliberate and calculated contribution to the allied war effort and one worthy of future consideration and recognition. For the French and British, and later the Russians, here was an unexpected source of assistance in a war where logistics, supply and co-ordination would be paramount.

The stage was set.

CHAPTER 13

AUSTRALIA GOES TO WAR

Back in Australia, the early recruiting drafts were very selective. They refused men with flat feet and bad teeth; they rejected Australians of Chinese heritage. The Defence Act of 1909 had specified that individuals who were 'not of substantial European origin or descent' would be exempt from joining for frontline duty. Added to this was the proviso that 'Only British subjects substantially of European origin should be recruited'. There were also physical requirements, but these were soon lowered as the demand for reinforcements increased. Short, small bodied Chinese men could now find a place in the ranks; various personal files list men of less than 5'2" (152cm).

Despite abuse and racism over many years and legislation aimed to prevent them joining up, the Chinese community rallied behind the nation's war effort. The Chinese press encouraged the enlistment of Chinese-Australians and took out advertisements encouraging the Chinese community to contribute to war loans. They also contributed to battalion comfort funds and raised money for the Red Cross and for welfare benefits for those returning wounded.

Men of Chinese ethnicity also joined the enlistment lines. Many were second and third generation native born Australians, who showed few features to indicate Chinese ancestry and had non-Chinese names. Of the 241 Chinese Australians who enlisted, 62 had Anglo-sounding names; there were 179, part of whose name, usually their surname, was Chinese.

While at times their Chinese heritage may have been obvious, many were probably known by the officers at the recruiting centres. The Australian Imperial Force (AIF) needed good men; both doctors and recruiting officers turned a blind eye to their ancestry. In the personal army files of these enlisting men, particularly under the heading, 'Distinctive Marks', there is no reference to any Chinese characteristics or physical features.

A typical recruit from the early days was George Griffiths, a Chinese-Australian from Victoria, who enlisted on 18 August 1914, just two weeks after the declaration of war. He was a miner aged 30, single, 5'7" tall, from Talbot, north of Ballarat. His battalion, the 8th, was formed in rural Victoria within a fortnight of the declaration of war. With his low serial number, Griffiths would have been an early recruit.

Griffiths left Melbourne in November 1914 and found himself in Egypt before landing at Gallipoli. He was in the attack at Krithia where his battalion suffered 217 casualties in one day, 8 May 1915. He was wounded soon afterwards and evacuated. In 1916, he went on to France, was gassed near Passchendaele, but recovered and returned to Australia in early 1919.

Others were not so lucky. Victor Lepp was one of three Chinese-Australian brothers who enlisted in 1915. They were from Ballarat, the descendants of Chinese miners. All three brothers went to Egypt, and Victor went on to Gallipoli and then to the Western Front. He was killed late in August 1916 at Poziéres when his battalion was 'engaged in carrying duties between the chalk pit and the frontline'. His two brothers returned to Australia in 1919.

Perhaps the most famous Chinese Anzac was William 'Billy' Sing, a horse driver who enlisted in Bowen in October 1914. Billy had been born to a Chinese father, John Sing, born in Shanghai and aged 44, and an English mother, Mary Ann Pugh aged 30 from Stafford in England. He had grown up in the bush, had left school at 12 and worked hard to support his family. He was tough, resourceful, could handle horses and was a great shot, attributes that would soon find a place in his dangerous and deadly life as a sniper.

The number of Chinese Anzacs who found themselves in Egypt and subsequently Gallipoli is not known, but it is probably small. Given the difficult medical requirements and 'origin' issues, young Chinese Australian volunteers, typically short in stature, with a small chest measurement, often frail-looking and of obvious Asian heritage, would have found enlistment difficult. Billy Sing was probably lucky: he was only 5'5" in height and 141 lbs in weight, just 63 kilograms.

Accepted into the 5th Light Horse Regiment, Billy found himself on the second convoy of troops destined for Egypt under the command of Brigadier-General Granville Ryrie, also known as 'The Bull'. He was a Boer War veteran and a man loved by his men. The Light Horsemen landed at Gallipoli on 20 May, the day after the massive attack of an estimated 40,000 Turks on the Australian line with over 10,000 casualties.

Billy soon went to work. He took up a sniping position at Chatham's Post; he moved around the frontline, often with his observer, Ion Idriess, later a noted author. His experience in the Queensland bush as a hunter and crack shot quickly brought him to the attention of his officers, first to General Birdwood, the Australian Commander, then to General Ian Hamilton, the Commander of the British forces on the Gallipoli peninsula, and finally to Lord Kitchener, the Secretary of State for War.

Billy's daily routine was simple and deadly. Having cleaned and oiled his rifle during the night, he and his observer would carefully make their way to his sniping position, lie down on a ground sheet, and begin their day's deadly work. Waiting and watching, the observer would carefully scan the Turkish trenches, less than 200 metres away; he would look for any movement, particularly around the small, brick-lined peep-holes that dotted the Turkish parapet. Once movement was detected, Billy would be guided to the spot and wait, his eye and rifle carefully sighted on the enemy trench. Then, a barely detectable movement and '*bang*', Billy had fired and another Turkish soldier lay dead in the bottom of the trench.

By the time he was evacuated from Gallipoli in November 1915, Bill Sing was officially credited with 201 kills. His commanding officer, Major Stephen Midgley DSO, believed it to be closer to 300. On 8 September 1915, Brigadier-General Ryrie recommended Billy Sing for a Distinguished Conduct Medal. When it was officially gazetted on 11 January 1916, the citation read:

For conspicuous gallantry from May to September 1915, at Anzac, as a sniper. His courage and skill were most marked and he was responsible for a very large number of casualties among the enemy, no risk being too great for him to take.

Another Chinese Anzac who served at Gallipoli was Nelson Sing from Claremont in Tasmania, but he does not appear to have been a relative of Billy Sing. He was 18 years old, just 5'3" tall, married and by trade a boat builder. He enlisted at Launceston in June 1915, went into the 26th Battalion and arrived at Gallipoli in September. He survived Gallipoli, but was wounded in the fighting at Poziéres in August 1916 and sent to England to recover from a gunshot wound to the leg.

Nelson Sing returned to France. He fought on with the 26th Battalion, through Bullecourt, the Menin Road and on to Passchendaele, the Battle of Amiens, Mont St Quentin and the Hindenburg Line. Sadly, he was killed in the very last Australian action in the French village of Montbrehain on 6 October 1918, just hours before the AIF was pulled out of the line and just five weeks before the end of the war.

Thanks to the work of Dr Edmond Chiu, Dr Sophie Couchman and the diligent researchers at the Chinese Museum in Melbourne, there have been 34 identified Chinese Anzacs who fought at Gallipoli. Four were killed in action, a further eight were wounded and two suffered from 'enteric' fever. This was in fact typhoid fever, a debilitating disease caused by poor sanitation, unclean food or infected water.

But inoculations kept the mortality rate low. The fever lasted from one to eight weeks.

With the final evacuation of Gallipoli in late December 1915, the Australians went first to Mudros on the island of Lemnos and then back to Egypt. Here the battalions from Gallipoli were split up to create new battalions: experienced men were mixed with new recruits from Australia. The AIF then continued a rigorous training programme and from March 1916 began transferring troops to the Western Front, first by ship from Alexandria to Marseilles and then by train to the operational areas around Armentiéres.

CHAPTER 14

BLOOD AND ATTRITION

The attrition rates for the Australians, and for all armies including the Germans, was very high. The attitude in Allied General Headquarters was simple: who would run out of men first, the Allies or the Germans? This problem of attrition refocused the minds of British and French commanders in their endless quest for more men to join the butcher's picnic.

With the growing need for men on one side and the generous offer of labourers from China on the other, negotiations moved quickly. In March 1915, the first discussions failed, but the increasingly static war, and the Allies' need to mobilise every possible man for the army, ensured the offer by Liang Shiyi was soon agreed to. In June 1915, Liang first offered Chinese help. French advisors had independently briefed the French Minister in Beijing, Alexandre Conty, to begin negotiations to recruit a Chinese labour force to assist the French war effort.

By November, further discussions had included the Chinese requirement that any Chinese recruited must be hired by a French contractor and not provided by the Chinese government. Conty was able to report to Paris that Liang had offered 30,000–40,000 workers. The French War Ministry accepted Liang's offer and dispatched a mission to China under Lieutenant Colonel Georges Truptil, which arrived in Beijing on 17 January 1916 and immediately set to work.

The Chinese government stipulated three conditions for the employment of Chinese labourers to the allied cause. First, the men could not be used for combat duties and must be kept clear of active, frontline areas. Second, the men would receive the same rights and conditions as French or British workers. Third, China reserved the right to send observers and government officials to ensure the men's rights and freedoms were being respected.

Though ostensibly 'agricultural', the work of the Truptil Mission soon came to the attention of the German minister for China, Admiral Hintze. Hintze reported to Berlin which in turned protested to the Chinese government that, even under the cover of a private contractor, this scheme was a breach of neutrality: one worker was equal to one soldier as a contribution to the Allied war effort. The Chinese response to Germany was that their nationals were free to work in Europe under contract and actually encouraged local governors and administrators to seek potential recruits in their provinces.

Issues began to arise very early in the French recruitment process; these would continue through various disputes and incidents for the duration of the war. In October 1916, the French tried to expand their concession by taking over a section of Tianjin which became known as the Laoxikai Incident. This, and other misunderstandings and disrespect of the Chinese by the French, caused serious disruptions in their recruiting plans and even attempts to draw men from southern China failed. In addition, the French civil and military administrations lacked co-ordination which further complicated, and in the end severely limited the number of Chinese working for the French army.

Britain had also been approached by Liang. As early as June 1915, Liang offered Chinese support, which was initially dismissed in London as impractical. However, like France, Britain had a manpower shortage; by early 1917, Britain needed to look for support further afield.

The British had already combed out men from industry and protected professions. They had replaced men with women in some cases. But more manual assistance would provide a fresh flush of manpower for the front. This was particularly where soldiers could be relieved from back areas behind the lines like ports, railways, factories and engineering works.

Both the threats and rumblings of British unionists and the racial concerns of the populace that were starting to be heard were ignored. In organising labour and manpower, the British believed, there lay the road to victory. No effort was to be spared in focusing the nation on essential war work.

Moreover, the spring and summer offensives in France, particularly the spectacularly bloody Battle of the Somme from July 1916, made Britain realise it had little choice but to accept the Chinese help.

Things began to move quickly in Britain. In parliament, Winston Churchill espoused the introduction of a Chinese labour force, claiming it would save British lives by contributing to the war effort. The Chinese 'coolie' was seen as an ideal worker: resilient, cheap to employ, tough and able to endure the northern winter, unlike black labour, which was seen as unfit for work in cold climates. So, in August 1916, Britain established its own recruiting organisation in China, not in Hong Kong as originally suggested, but in Weihaiwei on the Shandong Peninsula which, like the French initiative, began badly.

Unlike the French, the British did not use private contractors, but special agents of the British administration. Initial recruiting was slow. The British realised that they would need local Chinese support if the recruiting numbers were to increase. They negotiated a recruitment deal with the Chinese government. The deal included the suspension of reparations for 50 years, an agreement that would allow the raising of taxes and, most importantly, that Britain would support China in any peace agreement or conference at the conclusion of the war. By these means, Britain very quickly found itself with more Chinese labourers than did France. Labour units under British officers were well organised and under military control and organisation.

For both France and Britain, secrecy was of the utmost importance. Quite apart from issues of military secrecy, neither European nation liked the idea of being dependent on China for assistance. After the cruel and callous dealings over the previous 100 years, it was not a good image for Britain to portray. On the other hand, China was happy with this secrecy: it did not want either Japan or Germany to know of her involvement. The Chinese government was also embarrassed that traditionally her citizens left China on the threat of death but now, through international diplomacy and a view to the future, this was completely reversed, even legislated. It was hoped these men, sent far from home, might return to China with Western skills and know-how, even money to invest in small business enterprises and initiatives.

While the labourers destined for France were contracted by a nominal private company, the Chinese government indirectly controlled and monitored the workers' pay and conditions through a front organisation such as the Huimin Company. Under the French contract, labourers committed for five years, and were specifically employed for national defence, not military action. French law would protect their rights, allow them to practise their religion and provide for health care and holidays. Consideration was also given to the rations for the men (including 100 grams of rice per day) and appropriate clothing, bedding and cooking utensils. As a uniform, they were issued two sets of blue cotton suits, woollen trousers, a cardigan, waistcoat, raincoat, felt hat and a metal wrist band with their name and number.

Selecting men for the British Labour Corps was another thing. The British used the military physical inspection procedure: they accepted men between 20 and 40 years old, but rejected up to 60% of recruits for a range of medical conditions, including eye problems, venereal diseases, poor teeth and other physical impairments. Successful recruits were given a disinfectant bath, their heads were shaved and their pigtails removed, before they were issued their uniforms.

Finally, they were given a stamped metal disc around their wrist with a number and their name. It was to this number that payments were made by the pay office. They were also fingerprinted which was used to sign their contracts, prevent confusion and to create a reliable system of identification. Once passed physically, men went into barbed-wire enclosed camps (to prevent their escape) and undertook training that included marching and drills without weapons.

In comparison with the French, the British contract was less detailed, less favourable to the workers' needs and purposefully confusing. The Chinese labourer was contracted for three years rather than five and paid one French franc per day. Families received ten Chinese silver dollars per month. The British contracted labourers individually, not through a recruiting company, which made it hard for the Chinese to argue their rights or seek redress for non-compliance. Despite offering only modest payment for the dangerous work done, neither the French and English contracts made provision for pensions or realistic compensation for long term injury or disability until late in 1918. Even men killed or wounded by enemy shelling did not have a claim for compensation.

Another problem now confronted China: the care and support of these men far from home. While contracts included working conditions, pay rates and their legal rights, it was felt that these rights and conditions must be guaranteed by the presence of Chinese diplomatic staff to monitor and report on the workers progress and health. This highlighted problems. For instance the Chinese workers complained that the French were feeding them horse meat. The Chinese staff were well aware of the workers' predicament. On numerous occasions they complained, and protested human rights violations, mistreatment and contractual issues.

What was unexpected was the competition that quickly sprang up, particularly in northern China for strong, tall labourers. Both countries tried to resolve this by suggesting separate recruiting zones, but the problem went on until the cessation of recruiting in early 1918. Another problem was availability of shipping, particularly with the entry of America into the war.

Each country had made its own transport arrangements, but Britain had more ships available. The provision of British ships for French drafts of Chinese workers caused disputes: the French needed to rely on the British for transportation. So bad did this become that the French cancelled their recruitment programme in China in January 1918 and formally closed down the project the following month. With pressure also from

America for shipping, Britain cancelled the recruitment and transport of Chinese labourers two months later, in April 1918, in the knowledge that an extra 10,000 American troops could be transported to the front in the ships now available to the war effort.

In mid-1916, with the CLC now trained and ready, with transport available and an urgent need for extra manual labour on the Western Front, the first French contingents left China for France. By the end of 1917, the 'private' Chinese Huimin Company had recruited, processed, trained and shipped nearly 33,000 labourers of an estimated total of 40,000 who went to France. A further 95,000 went to Britain, although their plan had been to recruit a total of 150,000 for war service. Due to the limited availability of shipping, some labourers still in China had their contracts rescinded and were sent home.

It seems that approximately 140,000 Chinese labourers eventually made the long trip to France, but numbers may have been as high as 200,000. It is believed that between 200,000 and 500,000 went to Russia in a similar capacity, but estimates vary and the records have long gone. Whatever the exact number, this was the largest contingent of foreign labourers from any country who were employed by the Allies. What we know with certainty is that these Chinese men contributed greatly to the war effort, and in the process suffered from exhaustion, malnourishment, exposure, disease and even enemy action.

CHAPTER 15

THE BUTCHER'S PICNIC

By July 1916, the transfer of the Australians from Egypt was virtually complete. The Anzacs hated the heat, the sand and the filth. They were glad to find themselves on trains travelling north through the lush, green countryside of France for the battlefields beyond. As their trains passed Paris, the Eiffel Tower could be seen in the distance, but then it was not long before the distant rumble of the guns could be heard in the east.

Their train journey ended in northern France and from there they marched towards the front. Here they took up positions around Armentiéres in what was known as a 'nursery area', so-called because each side would send new, untried troops here to give them frontline experience without being shot at. This did not suit the way Australians operated. They soon started trench raids to annoy the Germans, but quickly found they were fighting a much more cunning enemy than Johnny Turk. The Germans whom the Australians found themselves fighting were a clever, well trained and aggressive adversary, in a land not of sand and searing heat, but of rain, mud and incessant artillery fire. It was a very different and deadly war.

The first Australian action was at Fromelles in July 1916. In 24 hours, there were 5,533 Australian casualties of whom 1,917 were killed. This is equivalent to the combined casualties in the Boer War, the Korean War and the Vietnam War. In this terrible engagement by the Australian 5th Division, there were nine Chinese Anzacs, two of whom were killed and one, who were wounded and captured. The battle was followed just four days later, on 23 July, by the first attack on Pozieres in which 32 Chinese Anzacs fought and a number were to die.

Meanwhile in Australia, the pressure for more men saw a lessening of standards and recruitment requirements. Age and height restrictions were lowered and many young Chinese-Australian men now found themselves eligible to enlist. There would also have been less interest shown in an Anglo-Chinese face. A number of Chinese-Australians enlisted and joined state-based battalions across the country. Now even men with an obvious Chinese heritage, with names like Tong, Shang and Loo Long, found they were acceptable.

Arthur Quong Tart was a case in point. He was from a wealthy merchant family in Sydney. His father, Mei Quong Tart had been a friend of the Australian George Ernest Morrison, the famous 'Morrison of

Peking' and *Times* of London correspondent, who had suggested him to the Emperor as the Chinese Consul in Sydney. His son Arthur was nearly 23 when he enlisted in August 1915. He was single, just five foot two inches tall and gave his occupation as a wool buyer. Arthur Quong Tart was posted to the 4th Machine Gun Company. He was wounded at Pozieres in late July 1916, soon after the attack was launched. The heavy, concentrated shelling, a continuous bombardment that was the most intense the Australians ever encountered in the Great War, decimated their ranks. Arthur Quong Tart was buried and dug out four times during his short stay in the line. He was sent to England to recover from 'shell shock', a disorder characterised by disorientation, tremors, panic and an inability to fight. It resulted from extended times under heavy shelling.

Recent research has found that shell shock is not primarily a psychological condition, as was first supposed, but includes damage to the brain tissue. Arthur Quong Tart's case was serious enough to see him declared medically unfit and he returned to Australia. He was discharged in Sydney in mid-1917.

In July 1915, 18-year-old postal worker, Royden Tong enlisted at Ballarat. He had a letter from his father giving him permission to enlist, which stated 'I hereby give my consent to my son Roy M. Tong to join the Australian Expeditionary Force for active service abroad', signed David Tong (146 Victoria Street, East Ballarat). Young Tong was wounded twice during his service, the first time in November 1916 in the mud northeast of Poziéres around Flers and Gueudecourt, and again in October 1917, when the fighting had moved north of the Menin Road towards Passchendaele, near Ypres in Belgium. Apart from losing 38 days pay for being Absent Without Leave, all we know of him is that he returned to Australia in April 1919 and disappeared.

While the demand for men now allowed the acceptance of Chinese-Australians into the ranks, it is apparent that not all men enlisting understood or trusted this at the time. Arthur Norman Tong, the younger brother of Royden Tong, also enlisted in February 1916 in Ballarat, but originally gave his name as Robert Arthur Bateson. There is a note in his personal file which simply reads: 'By sworn declaration assumed true name of Tong, Arthur Norman'. He survived the war and returned to Australia in September 1919.

During the Great War, nine men named Tong enlisted in the Australian Army. They were not all of Chinese origin. Two appear to be English. Frank Tong recorded his place of birth as Kingston in England, and was 5'7" tall with fair complexion and light brown hair. He was killed in action with the Light Horse at Gallipoli in late June 1915. The other was Thomas Tong, from Blackall in Queensland, who gave his place of birth as Middlesex England. He was a 25-year-old motor driver, 5'9" tall with a fair complexion and hair. He was to die of wounds in the terrible fighting on the Broodseinde ridge just below Passchendaele village. Despite their distinctly Chinese name, but being tall and fair, neither was likely to be of Chinese heritage.

Also enlisting at this time were two brothers, Caleb Duckbour Shang and Sidney Wah Shang. Caleb was the eldest of 13 children, born in Brisbane in 1884. Sidney was the fifth child and born in Rockhampton in 1891. While working as a labourer in Innisfail, Sid decided to enlist. He had distinct Chinese features, so he travelled to Cairns where he was unknown and perhaps would have a better chance. He was accepted in January 1916 and went into the 12th Battalion, but when his brother also tried to enlist in Cairns, he was rejected.

Caleb was 34 at the time and working as a clerk in Babinda. After being rejected in Cairns, he travelled instead to Brisbane where he was accepted into the AIF on 5 June 1916. Australia had cause to be grateful for his persistence. He sailed from Australia with the 47th Battalion in September 1916 and, for his part in the fighting at Messines in June 1917, an action the Australian Official Historian Charles Bean mentions in the *Official History*, he was awarded the Distinguished Conduct Medal.

His citation read:

For conspicuous gallantry and devotion to duty on numerous occasions. He acted as runner continuously for four days through barrages and fire swept areas, carrying water, food and ammunition to the front line. He attacked enemy snipers in broad daylight and accounted for them. In addition to this, he constantly volunteered for dangerous patrols into enemy country, where he gained valuable information as a scout, and also showed remarkable skill in improvising lamp signals in a very dangerous position whence he could send information to Battalion Headquarters. His conduct showed a never-failing example of fearlessness, resource and initiative.

Caleb Shang was again in action at Dernancourt where a gallant defence by the Australians stopped the German advance. He was awarded a bar to his DCM (a second DCM). His citation for the action noted:

For conspicuous gallantry and devotion to duty at DERNANCOURT on April 5th 1918 and previous *occasions. This soldier's example has always been a source of pride in this Battalion, but on this occasion, he excelled himself by his wonderful powers of endurance, intrepidity and utter contempt for danger. He volunteered for an O.P. (Observation Post) in an advanced position at the start of operations and maintained it throughout until attack started when he reaped a harvest with his rifle until his post was blown right out. He came back through enemy fire to get more rifles but was employed as runner and made several trips through enemy barrage which was intense. He continued carrying ammunition and running until company moved out when he volunteered to remain behind and cover retirement with a Lewis Gun which he did successfully. He showed an utter disregard for danger and is a gallant soldier.*

Shang was again in the thick of the action at Villers Bretonneux for which he was awarded a Military Medal. His citation for this action read:

At VILLERS BRETONNEUX on 1st May, 1918, he displayed remarkable bravery and initiative in making a daylight reconnaissance of the Sector under heavy Machine Gun fire and snipers' activities and which proved of considerable value to us. He established an O.P. at which he was continually sniped at and succeeded in conveying back valuable information of enemy movement and directed our artillery fire on to the enemy formations causing them many casualties. He maintained this Post during tour in line without relief.

On 16 August 1918, Shang was wounded during the Allied advance in the Battle of Amiens and was sent to England to recover. He remained in hospital until he embarked for Australia in December, returning to a hero's welcome in Cairns, the town in which he was not accepted for enlistment. He is among the most decorated Australians of the First World War and the most decorated Chinese digger. There is also evidence that he was considered for the Victoria Cross.

Meanwhile, his younger brother Sidney Wau Shang, who had enlisted in early January 1916, joined his battalion in September. They had been part of the Australian attack on Mouquet Farm near Pozieres. During the terrible winter of 1916–17, he suffered from trench feet, the freezing of the lower legs and feet. He was admitted to hospital. In September 1917, he attended a cooking course and remained with his battalion until his return to Australia in August 1919.

Despite Caleb Shang's decorations, probably the most famous Chinese Anzacs after Billy Sing were the Langtip brothers from Tarraville in rural Victoria. In January 1916, six brothers travelled to Melbourne to enlist together, but given the concern that so many from one family were going to war, initially three and then two, were sent home. The four who finally found themselves in the Light Horse were Henry aged 27, Ernest aged 22, Leslie aged 20 and Bertie aged 19. They all joined the 4th Light Horse then transferred to the Camel Corps. All four brothers returned home. In all, there were 15 Chinese Anzacs in the Light Horse, including the Langtip boys and Billy Sing.

Of the brothers, Leslie drew the most attention. He rode in the famous Light Horse charge at Beersheba and was to be awarded a DCM in the advance on Kaukab on 30 September 1918. His citation read:

'This NCO gave valuable assistance in the capture of a field gun and showed great initiative and courage. He forced the enemy drivers to take their gun towards our lines under heavy fire and when a party of the enemy endeavoured to retake the gun, he took up a position and drove back the party.'

In another interesting incident, just outside Damascus, there is a great story of this young Chinese Anzac coming upon an English officer berating his

Arab troops. Leslie tells the Englishman what he thinks of his attitude and when the Englishman ignores him, he stepped forward and 'punched him on the nose'. Little did he know at the time that the officer, Colonel Thomas Edward Lawrence, was indeed the famous 'Lawrence of Arabia'.

Across the Western Front, Anzacs of Chinese ancestry were contributing to the war effort. Many of the early enlistments were introduced to the Western Front to take part in the terrible fighting for the French village of Poziéres from July to September 1916. It began on 23 July when the Australians attacked Poziéres after the failure of British attempts to take the village. They quickly overran the German defenders, capturing the blockhouse (Gibraltar), and fanning out through the village and up towards the important Windmill site on the high ground to the northeast.

Killed in the early stages of the attack was Charles You, a 24-year-old married carter in the 11th Battalion. His personal file says he was killed in the period 22–25 July 1916, no doubt in the intense shelling put down on the village once the Australians had occupied the southern part. The Battalion War Diary states:

'On the 25th instant from about 6.30am to 6pm, our lines were intensively bombarded ... by the enemy. The greater parts of our works were destroyed and the ruins of Poziéres were completely changed. We suffered very heavy casualties although we had our lines thinned to the bare minimum ... During the whole of the operations we were subjected to rifle fire from our right and right rear and the enemy shelled incessantly.'

In this action, the battalion lost seven officers and 153 men killed, and 11 officers and 358 men wounded. 'In the face of intense fire, parties worked with great resolution although suffering many casualties'. They were relieved on the night of 25/26 by the 19th Battalion. By the time it was withdrawn, the 11th Battalion had suffered 529 casualties, including 160 officers and men killed.

As they pushed forward, the Australians finally took the high ground above the village at what is known as the Windmill site. Today a stone plinth notes:

The ruin of Poziéres windmill which lies here was the centre of the struggle in this part of the Somme battlefield in July and August 1916. It was captured on August 4th by Australian troops who fell more thickly on this ridge than on any other battlefield of the war.

It was here that another Chinese Anzac fell. His name was George Sheck, a jockey born in Echuca on the Murray River who enlisted in Bendigo. He was just 5'4½" tall, but old by the standards of the time, at 37 years of age. He was in the 22nd Battalion, and along with another Chinese Anzac, Edward James King, was to be killed on this bloody slope.

The battalion's records show that both men came up from the rear and were working close to Poziéres in carrying parties and digging trenches. They moved into the line on the outskirts of Poziéres on 4 August 1916 and immediately came under heavy artillery fire. During the night, the Germans counter-attacked this newly won position at the Windmill, but were beaten back leaving 200 dead in front of the Australian trenches.

The following day, 5 August, the 22nd Battalion consolidated its position just in time for a second German attack on their line. This attack forced the Australians back. The Australians counter-attacked, and re-took the position, but not before 75% of the attacking Germans were cut down and left scattered across the battlefield. The position, so important to the Allied advance, had held. But, owing to the severity of the artillery fire and the casualties, the battalion was withdrawn on 6 August and returned to Sausage Valley behind the line.

For this brief time in the line, the battalion suffered very badly, with 651 casualties (of about 900 who went in) of whom 238 were killed. Among them were George Sheck and Edward King, their bodies lost on that terrible, bloody ridge. Today their names are on the wall of the Australian National Memorial at Villers Bretonneux, just two of nearly 11,000 names of Australians with no known grave in the Somme battlefields.

One other Chinese Anzac was also to die in the fighting at Poziéres. His name was Walter Quan who had enlisted at Blackboy Hill camp in Perth in August 1915. He was a miner from Meekatharra in outback Western Australia who was allocated to the reinforcements sent to the 16th Battalion in Egypt. The AIF wanted to include experienced men in the new battalions that were being formed, by splitting in half the Gallipoli battalions and forming a new unit. Walter Quan found himself in the 'daughter' battalion of the 16th: the 48th. Commanded by Lieutenant Colonel Ray Leane, this battalion was jokingly known as the 'Joan of Arc Battalion' (she was known as the Maid of Orleans) because it was said to be 'made of all Leanes.' There were a number of family members in the battalion.

Walter moved towards the front line and, on 4 August 1916, crossed Tara Hill just east of the town of Albert. From here he would have seen the frightening horizon ahead, lit by flares and endless explosions and flashes of light. It would have been terrifying to know that just ahead was this frightful cauldron of gas, fire and death. Every step took you closer. After remaining in Sausage Valley for a few days, Walter moved forward, past Casualty Corner, along the sunken road known to the men as Deadman's Road, past the infamous Poziéres chalk pit, across Pioneer Trench and into the line at Tramway Trench, just below the Windmill.

The ground was open and exposed, so men and supplies needed to go forward without cover and under heavy fire. Here the 48th Battalion was to take nearly 600 casualties out of a battalion strength of some 900 men. Walter Quan was one of them. His body was recovered and buried in the Serre Road Cemetery No. 2 near Beaumont Hamel north of Poziéres. This cemetery contains 699 Australians, 370 of them 'Known unto God' as their headstone says, all but a few from the fighting at Poziéres.

CHAPTER 16

ACROSS THE SEAS

Like many of the Australian diggers from the bush, many Chinese labourers had never seen a ship, let alone the open sea. They were, however, excited by their selection and training and being part of China's special contribution to the Allied war effort. Whether east or west, their journey would be difficult, extremely uncomfortable and dangerous.

From China, some travelled across the Pacific to Vancouver where they boarded a train for the 6,000 kilometre train journey to the east coast and then another ship across the Atlantic to Britain or France. Others turned west, heading for Cape Town and the Atlantic, or through the Suez Canal, the Mediterranean and on to the ports of southern France like Marseilles, from where they took the train north.

From the beginning, transporting a Chinese workforce to the European battlefields was a difficult undertaking. This was made more difficult when the Germans declared their unrestricted submarine campaign in February 1917, which had been earlier suspended after the sinking of the *Lusitania*. The trip across the Pacific was free of the submarine threat, but both the Atlantic and the Mediterranean were hunting grounds for the German submarine fleet. This was soon to have a major impact on China.

In March 1917 the Canadian government received a request from the British government to introduce and manage the passage of an unspecified number of Chinese labourers across Canada for transhipment from various east coast ports. This would be paid for by the British but managed and secured by the Canadians. The first group arrived on the *Empress of Russia* in early April 1917. On arrival, they were medically checked, issued clothes, food and bedding, and placed on board carriages of the Canadian Pacific Railway Company. This was the first of many trainloads of Chinese labourers for the next year or so. Not only were the men sent by train to the east, but after the war, they also followed the same route in reverse for their return trip to China.

The plan, however, had its problems. To tranship Chinese labourers by rail across Canada in secret required concealment of the men while leaving the port, boarding the train and travelling across Canada and onto a ship at an east coast port such as Montreal or Halifax, and even American ports like St John. This required very strict security, special guard detachments, a close watch on letters and telegrams and the censorship of the Canadian press. Attempts were also made to ensure the American press did not publish stories, but this was not always successful.

Apart from the dangers of enemy action and the weather, the passage on the ships and the railway was very uncomfortable and unhealthy. Men were crammed in, provided only hammocks and chairs to sleep on and given basic rations, including rice. On some ships, safety standards were lowered and both lifeboats and personal life vests reduced. This was encouraged by the British authorities, who offered excuses about rationing, availability of supplies and the pressures of war. They ignored the element of human safety in a way which highlighted their attitude to those whom they saw as simply 'coolie' labour.

At this time in Canada, there was a tax of $500 on Chinese wishing to enter the country, an enormous amount of money at the time. Canadian legislation aimed to prevent the entry of Chinese people. Those in Canada, staying on after the construction of the railways, found discrimination against them everywhere apparent. The transiting Chinese workers were treated poorly, and their passage was secured only after strict conditions of secrecy and security were imposed.

The Canadians also feared that the transiting Chinese labourers would interact with Chinese then living in Canada for espionage purposes. Railcars were locked and a guard mounted to prevent escape. The CLC men were virtual prisoners. Complaints were raised at the time about this ill-treatment, but nothing seems to have come of it. Exercise time to stretch arms and legs was limited; there were insufficient medical supplies to treat those getting sick or injured along the way. However, not all Canadians were hostile. At times, local ladies auxiliaries organised welcome parties and provided fruit and small gifts, but in general, the Chinese were ignored and disliked.

Upon arrival in France, the Chinese were sent to either French or British camps. In each case, they came under the control of the military: their daily lives, their discipline and management were undertaken along proven military lines. This included mail delivery, which was controlled by the military, and censorship of mail, both to and from China. The authorities feared divulging to those at home military or strategic information to the enemy, and their treatment and conditions at the front. They were forbidden to send newspaper cuttings, postcards or photographs and were only allowed to send two letters per month to their families.

Immediately upon arrival in France, the CLC men were formed into working battalions of 500 men under a British officer. These officers were generally second-rate, young, wounded or incapacitated. Rarely did they have any Chinese language skills, and even the translators supplied were inexperienced and poor. The failure of these officers to direct the work properly or to communicate what was required, severely hampered the efficiency of the Corps. It resulted in poor quality work and low morale. A Chinese-English phrase book was written and distributed, but it did little to help.

Nevertheless, the Chinese were soon hard at work. Many of the Chinese labourers were sent to French factories and government agencies well behind the line. Those Chinese serving with the British found themselves behind the firing line, but still within the danger zone of long-range German artillery.

Then in 1918, German Gotha bombers ranged far behind the lines: they bombed camps, supply depots and coastal ports. In raids on Boulogne and Dunkirk on 1 and 5 September 1917, 15 labourers were killed and a further 21 injured. On 18 May 1918, an air raid killed up to 60 Chinese. There were also casualties from gas attacks and from long-range German shelling of supply areas and train lines, places where Chinese camps were located. All this despite the fact that placing members of the CLC within danger was in breach of their contracts and also affected their commitment and productivity.

Despite the discrimination and poor treatment they suffered, the Chinese labourers' hard work and commitment soon came to the attention of the Allies. The Allied authorities were surprised at what they could achieve; how industrious they were; how clever in solving engineering problems and achieving results. It was noted that they were capable of heavier work and greater results than British Labour units or those from the Commonwealth like South Africa, India or Egypt. Often comparisons were made, for example in the production of duckboards. It was found that Chinese gangers virtually ran the tank workshops, so proficient were the Chinese work teams. They were also noted for working hard over a ten-hour day and were selected by both the French and the British over all other colonial labourers.

As the war continued, the CLC found themselves doing a wide range of jobs. Roads needed constant maintenance, particularly in winter, which meant heavy work with road base and other materials. By the coast, the Chinese loaded and unloaded ships and trains, repaired the running rails and signal equipment, washed and serviced tanks and trucks and maintained power and telegraph wires.

In French areas, they worked in munition, paper and acid factories, arsenals and warehouses and in government establishments and repositories. Most of all, they dug miles and miles of trenches and undertook a range of engineering works like concrete emplacements, gun positions and the building of Nissen huts. Most importantly for the war effort, they released Allied soldiers from labouring tasks to fighting units at a time when, as General Haig said, they had 'their backs to the wall'.

CHAPTER 17

THE END OF HOSTILITIES

Within the Australian army, men of Chinese heritage were also well regarded. In all, about 250 men of Chinese heritage are believed to have fought with the AIF during the First World War and 46 were killed in action or died of wounds or sickness.

With the ending of hostilities, little changed for the Chinese labourers on the Western Front. They had perhaps a day free after the announcement of the end of hostilities, probably more due to the absence of their British officer, somewhere drunk and mentally absent. They would not have felt the friendship of the French or Belgium people, enjoyed the street celebrations, the hugs and kisses of the girls or drunk their fill of wine, beer or cider. They would have been removed from this, probably caged up and ignored. Yet it was their victory also.

Now the Chinese labourers were faced with another task: clearing up the battlefields and working towards restoring France and the countryside to that which existed before 1914. Quickly the French and Belgians, the British and the Americans, turned against the Chinese. Racism emerged at a level not seen before, attitudes changed and the Chinese were blamed for accidents and crimes in which they had no involvement.

To compound this, the YMCA and the British officers who had looked after their welfare and working conditions returned home. Friction grew between those who remained and the labourers. While they too wanted to go home, there was much to do. After General Pershing refused to allow American troops to do this work, even though many had been in France only a few months, they all returned home. There were, therefore, very few other manual labourers available to do the work.

Instead of working at the Channel ports, which would have best satisfied the terms of the contracts, the CLC under British military control were moved inland to the devastated areas of the battlefields. Here they were directed to collect barbed wire, fill in trenches, clear away dangerous ordinance and recover bodies. Untrained, they found themselves dealing with booby traps, unexploded shells and explosives, all of which took a terrible toll over the next few years.

These men worked until 1920 in the British areas and until 1922 in French areas. The CLC men were the very last British forces to leave France. During their time in Europe, the lowest estimates of fatalities is about 2,000; recent Chinese research puts the figure at 10,000 and even as high as 20,000. Part of the death toll included around 800 Chinese who were lost at sea, either working on British-registered ships or as casualties of German submarine attacks. The greatest loss of life in this regard was the sinking of the French passenger ship *Athos*, near Malta in the Mediterranean, where 543 CLC men on their way to France lost their lives.

With the close of hostilities, each man received a service medal from the British (93,357 were handed out) but it was back to work. Because of their neglect of duty or misconduct, a few man missed out on a medal. Probably more important was the fact that at an award ceremony, a British officer from China told the men, 'By your faithful and loyal service you have upheld the best traditions of China and have formed a closer relationship between the East and the West'.

Little else, however, was said by way of thanks or gratitude for the suffering and pain these men had endured, nor for the racism, the neglect and the sacrifice. In the elation and exultation of the moment, in the joy and rapture of victory, these men were already forgotten. Thus it would remain.

Some 7,000 men, however, found a new life in France. Many worked at the Renault car plant; others opened restaurants serving Chinese cuisine. This became the genesis of the Chinese population in Europe: many heirs of these original Chinese labourers remain in France today. The French were far less racist than the British. They more readily accepted of Oriental ways and were prepared to offer rights similar to those granted to French workers.

Of the foreign workers who aided the Allied cause, the Chinese were considered the hardest working, the most co-operative and the most valuable. General Foch, the Supreme Commander is quoted: 'They were first class workers who could be made excellent soldiers, capable of exemplary bearing under modern artillery fire'.

Yet with all their input and sacrifice, once the war was over there was little recognition of the Chinese contribution. They had proved more efficient and productive than labour corps from other Empire nations, but they received few war medals. The British government even tried to reduce their pension money. Not only did the Europeans ignore their wartime contribution, they were blamed for the introduction of the Spanish flu. There is recent evidence that the influenza pandemic of 1917–1920, which killed an estimated 50 million people, did have its origin in China and may have been brought to Europe by the Chinese labourers. The CLC were also blamed for general instability and disturbances behind the frontline, a totally false claim given their virtually crime-free record.

CHAPTER 18

GOING HOME

Following the war and their experience with the CLC, the dominant belief among European minds was that the Chinese were inferior human beings. They had shown their resourcefulness and imagination in many instances, but they were not their mental equal. The Europeans did not take into account the problems of language and communication, including the fact that there were very few interpreters to assist the management of these non-English speaking men. In addition, the British and French often posted officers unsuitable for other appointments to the CLC units. It is no surprise that they proved poor managers of men, yet it was the men of the CLC who were blamed for this incompetence.

The British, in particular, were often brutal and unjust in their punishment of CLC labourers. They remained ignorant of Chinese sensibilities and customs; misunderstandings were compounded by the lack of clear communication. They imposed military courts, harsh sentences, beatings and even execution. There was also a chaotic administration operating above the CLC, with no communication between the Chinese recruiting centres and the CLC Headquarters run by Colonel Fairfax in France.

Punishment, rather than good management, was seen as the way to control the Chinese. As a result, the Chinese held demonstrations and strikes. They refused to take orders, which led in turn to mass arrests and even instances where the guards opened fire, killing strikers. Suicides among the Chinese became more frequent. They were treated like prisoners, given few means of entertainment or of relieving their boredom and not allowed to visit nearby villages or mix with the local people.

The French treated their Chinese labourers far better, particularly after the war. They were free to leave their camps, go to cafes and bars and even enjoy the company of local prostitutes. The French run CLC camps were often in open rural areas, without barbed wire enclosures and guards. Men were tightly packed in living quarters, but there were few restrictions placed on them outside working hours.

The French also provided judicial protection. They allowed Chinese workers to take French civilians and military personnel to court for ill-treatment. Some Chinese stole away from British labour units and re-appeared in French units, such was the difference in discipline and working conditions. The French too showed their disciplinary side: there were also cases of Chinese workers being abused, beaten and even killed. Similarly, not all British units were harsh. There were units where the British officers after the war were celebrated and thanked by their Chinese labourers.

One cultural problem that arose was that, should they happen to die in Europe, the Chinese wanted their bodies returned to China. This was naturally difficult for the British authorities at a time when all British and Empire dead were buried where they fell in France and Belgium. But it was a matter of grave importance to the Chinese, who needed to be returned to their own land so that they might pass on to Heaven.

To resolve this, the British provided individual graves for the labourers, plus funeral clothing, coffins and a headstone. They established a Chinese cemetery at Noyelles-sur-Mer in France, at a site chosen by the Chinese after it was approved and blessed by the feng shui master. At burials, a coffin draped with the Union Jack was carried by Chinese pall bearers, and the service overseen and reported on by a British medical officer.

In a similar way, the British ensured the Chinese had satisfactory medical help. A hospital was set up at Noyelles, with the latest equipment and facilities including an X-ray machine and with well-equipped operating theatres, staffed by Chinese medical staff. It had been determined early that the Chinese labourers must have the same quality of care and hospital facilities as a British soldier. This was generally the case. When it opened in 1917, the Noyelles hospital had 1,500 beds, 16 foreign doctors and 300 nurses and other medical staff. It was able to handle mental patients, those with various eye problems, and even leprosy.

Now, the civilians who had been displaced by the war returned to their home towns, villages and farms. They reacted against the Chinese visitors. The locals feared them, disliking their clothes and their eating habits, their language and, as the Europeans saw it, their potential for violence. Pressure was placed on the CLC to return their men to China, particularly the sick. This prompted a chaotic response, suddenly rounding up and returning whole units of Chinese labourers to coastal ports and from there onto ships, the Canadian railway and on to China, still in their filthy clothes and in their sick and unhygienic state. This naturally proved very embarrassing to the labourers and ultimately to their families.

However, men returned with savings from their years of labour. This went towards opening small businesses, building a house or bettering their social position. They also returned with a view and understanding of the outside world. On the one hand, the war left deep scars and memories of intolerance, abuse and contempt. On the other, the men of the CLC gained new expectations and visions. This alone injected a new enthusiasm, confidence and motivation in the dawning light of the changed nation.

The greatest regret for China was the betrayal they felt at the Versailles Peace Conference, which began on 18 January 1919. The Allies completely ignored China's contribution and that of the thousands of Chinese men who served the Allied cause.

The Chinese sent a delegation of 62 officials. But in the end, only two received a place at the table, unlike their enemy Japan who had five seats. On 28 January, the Chinese delegate Wellington Koo gave a passionate speech to the assembly, demanding that the German concession at Tsingtao be returned to China, not Japan, and that colonial concessions be revoked.

Despite promises of support from Britain for the withdrawal of the Japanese forces from Tsingtao, the Chinese found no friends on the Allied side, especially President Wilson of the USA. They were shocked and humiliated when Article 156 gave Japan control of Shandong Province. This, they argued, was the birthplace of Confucius and the 'cradle of Chinese civilisation' but to no avail. In desperation, they walked out of the Conference.

These humiliations were keenly felt at home. Across China there were demonstrations, and the Chinese government was bombarded with petitions and demands for this to be overturned. Fortunately for China, at the Washington Naval Conference in 1922, the United States mediated these difficult issues, and sovereignty over Shandong Province was returned to China. The Japanese were forced to withdraw. On 19 July 1919, along with contingents from 18 other nations, the Chinese did attend the massive victory parade in London.

CHAPTER 19

ARMISTICE AND A NEW WORLD

The Armistice on 11 November 1918 saw the AIF playing a new role. Their last action had been at Montbrehain on 6 October, where the long serving Nelson Sing was killed in action. After this, the AIF were withdrawn to rest areas in the rear and took no further part in the fighting. Many were taken by surprise when an Armistice was called and the fighting ceased. Even the rowdy celebrations of the French civilians were not enough to convince them and many waited for the English newspapers to arrive before they believed the war had finally ended.

By war's end, it is believed a total of 46 Chinese Australians were killed serving in the AIF. While they made up a tiny proportion of the 330,000 Australians who went to war, they certainly gave their all: 19 Chinese Anzacs were awarded medals for bravery and devotion to duty.

But what now? While the men saw it as a simple matter to go back to England and take the first ship to Australia, the reality was very different. Not only was there a shortage of ships available to return

Allied soldiers to their home countries — America, Canada, India, South Africa, and New Zealand — but Australian Prime Minister Billy Hughes demanded that comfortable ships be provided for the AIF for their return, with well-aired bunkrooms, fresh food and an orchestra or band to entertain the troops on the long voyage home.

Of course, these ships were not readily available. So the men stayed first in Europe, ready if Germany should decide to resume the war, and then were slowly withdrawn back to the Australian camps on the Salisbury Plain in England, a very familiar site to most of them. This became home and from where they went on leave. They travelled around the United Kingdom on free rail passes or to a number of educational or trade courses under a broad education training scheme headed by General Monash. Many men undertook basic literacy skills, learnt trades like motor mechanics, wool classing and bricklaying; others went to factories and offices, some even to the USA, to learn specialist skills and trades.

During this time, the Chinese Anzacs would not have been treated any differently from the Australian diggers. While the camps in England were dreary, tedious and wearisome, the question was: 'when are we going home?' Many men took the time to travel and fraternise with the local English girls, and many men married; an estimated 6,000 marriages took place. This caused an extra burden on the transport authorities, as now wives and children of AIF men had also to be returned to Australia.

Billy Sing had met and married Elizabeth Stewart, a waitress from Edinburgh on one such trip. She was 21, ten years younger than Billy and, apart from details of their marriage in late June 1917, she did not return to Australia. She disappeared into obscurity.

Like so many veterans who returned in 1918 and 1919, Billy came home to a very different Australia. All faced a lack of work prospects, educational opportunities and indifference to their service and sacrifice. To be of Chinese, or even slightly Asian appearance, would not have helped and although we know very little about the circumstances of the Chinese Anzacs, we can be sure that both their opportunities and their future prospects would have been grim.

Men like Billy Sing, for all their decorations and fame, found there was little for them in Australia on their return. Billy's marriage was short-lived. He was briefly feted as an Anzac hero, but he soon slipped into obscurity. He returned to the bush and the trades he had known: he worked on remote stations or as a gold prospector but never struck it rich. He died in obscurity during the Second World War and was buried in a pauper's grave in Lutwyche Cemetery in Brisbane.

While the Chinese Anzacs fighting with the AIF had earned the high regard of their mates, this was not the case in society at large and among the Chinese community in Australia. The White Australia policy was principally enacted to prevent non-white immigration. It also held pernicious clauses that affected the Australian-Chinese population already in the country. Socially they were barely accepted, made to feel unwelcome and outcast. Now, they were also legislated against.

The biggest discrimination came in the form of employment opportunities. Chinese workers were slowly given notice and let go from Commonwealth jobs and the mining industry. Many jobs were made unavailable to them: mail delivery, work in transport or joining the public service. Chinese Australians were also excluded from business enterprises. They were unable to establish a company or purchase land, and they could not be naturalised. Australia was not a happy place for even long-established Chinese residents or for those who served.

CHAPTER 20

THE FORGOTTEN

China had committed to the Allied side in August 1917, declaring war on Germany. It did so on the understanding it would have a place in the post-war peace talks. The Armistice was celebrated by a massive victory parade in Beijing: 60,000 people took to the streets. China expected to be able to take a new place in the post-war world. The Chinese also hoped that the Fourteen Point Plan offered by US President Woodrow Wilson would form the basis of a new world order and a positive resolution of the Japanese occupation problem.

China, however, was caught in a cleft stick. The Western powers realised that forcing Japan from her Chinese concessions, like the province of Shandong, would also compromise their own concessions. China was weak and could do little to influence or alter the trading concessions, but the increasing military and naval power of the Japanese was altogether a different matter. In the end, Japanese intransigence won. When details of what was seen as an American betrayal reached China, there were widespread demonstrations and public denunciations of the US. The gate was flung open to the rise of a new nationalism and a new political direction: Communism.

China not only came out of the war unrecognised and unrewarded for her contribution, but in one instance, actually painted out of history.

In September 1914, work began on an enormous circular panoramic painting known as the 'Pantheon de la Guerre'. It was 402 feet (123 metres) in circumference and 45 feet (14 metres) high, the largest painting in the world. It was worked on by up to 130 artists who depicted some monumental events of the First World War and included all the Allied nations, including the CLC. However, when the Americans entered the war and the painting was almost complete, there was no room on the vast canvas for them to be represented and included. So it was decided to paint out the CLC men and replace them with Americans. This says so much and is why we wish today to remember the Forgotten.

The outbreak of the Second World War again saw Chinese Australians fight for the country. Recent research reveals that some 600 men and women of Chinese ancestry joined the 2nd AIF, the Royal Australian Navy, the Royal Australian Airforce and women's auxiliary units during the course of the war. They also served in the merchant navy, support units and formations within Australia.

Today little is known of the Chinese men who fought for their country. These men put aside the abuse and racism they and their families had endured since their arrival in Australia.

Credit and thanks are owed to the efforts of the Chinese Museum in Melbourne and to dedicated staff and volunteers like Emeritus Professor Dr Edmond Chiu, Dr Sophie Couchman, Chinese Museum Curator Ms Joyce Agee and the staff at the Australian War Memorial in Canberra. Only for the research and investigation undertaken by these dedicated volunteers, are these servicemen, like the thousands of workers in the Chinese Labour Corp, remembered.

Lest we forget.

POSTSCRIPT

Albert Yue Ling Wong AM

In the preceding chapters, Dr Will Davies has provided us with a glimpse of the historical background, the context and the mindset of China and the European nations up until the Great War.

For over one hundred years, European powers, in particular, Britain, France and Germany, exploited China's weaknesses. They sought to broaden their trading spheres of influences, extend import and export trade and, in the process, to impose Western ways, technology and democracy. In vying for their slice of China, they created internal self-inflicted turmoil, revolution, national humiliation and effected a total breakdown of the traditional order.

This in turn saw the Chinese leaving their homeland for greener pastures. They tried their luck for a better life in America, Canada and Australia as miners, service providers and railway builders. But they were not always welcomed: they had trouble assimilating and their value was questioned.

With the onset of the First World War, there was a need for physical labour to replace frontline soldiers. It suited the British, French and Russian governments to exploit the cheap Chinese labourers, just as they had exploited China for the previous 100 years. To satisfy this demand, these men, simply 'coolies' in their eyes, came mostly from the northern Chinese province of Shandong where there was excess labour and a lack of work.

As Dr Davies has outlined, it suited China politically to provide this tacit support to the allies. China was not directly engaged in the First World War and at that point remained neutral. We have read of the Chinese Labour Corps and of the 241 Australians of Chinese heritage who enlisted into the Australian Imperial Forces (AIF). Despite the racism and the challenges of the time, these men fought and gave their all, side by side with their Anglo-Saxon brothers.

As I stated in the Preface, I wanted this relatively unknown chapter in our history reinstated for the benefit of the younger and future generations of Australians, especially those of Chinese ethnicity. With a better understanding of Chinese participation and sacrifice, we stand a better chance of a more inclusive and cohesive society, a better Australia where Chinese migrants and those of other ethnicities can feel a sense of belonging, in particular when it comes to sacred dates in our calendar such as Anzac Day and Armistice Day. It is my strong personal belief that understanding this unknown and forgotten chapter of history will better allow migrants to assimilate, integrate, to embrace Australian values and our way of life.

More recently, there have been reports in the media about Chinese influence in Australian society. It is not in Australia's long-term interests to disengage from our major trading partner, from what is the region's most influential player for the foreseeable future.

Let me indulge for a moment. The bonds of friendship between Australia and China go back centuries and Chinese influence is not new. In 2018, we celebrated the 200th anniversary of the first official Chinese settler in Australia: a Chinese carpenter, Mak Sai Ying, settled in Sydney in 1818. He worked for several prominent families of the time, and went on to become the owner of a hotel. Mr Mak was the first of many Chinese who have made Australia their home. According to his great-grandson Barry Shying, Mak Sai Ying, aka John Shying, had four children, all sons. It is believed they ran a funeral parlour in George Street, Sydney. One grandson, named Martin, the father of Barry Shying, was born in 1886, worked for the large car distributor Harden and Johnston and passed away in 1942 when Barry was only ten years old.

Barry grew up in Marrickville in inner Sydney, went to school locally and moved interstate when he was nineteen. Barry Shying knew nothing of his Chinese ancestry until he was approached during the Bicentennial in 1988. As he says, he, and no one in his family show any Chinese features so it came as some surprise to find he had Chinese forebears and in fact, a great-great grandfather who is today recognised as the first Chinese migrant.

Barry Shying has four children, two sons and two daughters. His grandson Nicholas, an arts-law student at Monash University, now carries forward the family name but as Barry says, other Shyings are most likely in Sydney or within Australia. This is a wonderful link. It stretches back 200 years to the earliest days of the colony and, in the process, shows the contribution of the family and its history springing from this humble man.

Yet even before this, Chinese influence has been present for a very long time, possibly as far back as the 18th century. Aboriginal rock art in the Northern Territory depicts Macassan sailors from Indonesia harvesting sea cucumbers for the China trade. Chinese Qing Dynasty coins, minted from 1736 and 1795, have been found on islands off the coast of Australia.

Later history, however, suggests that this influence went both ways. At the turn of the 20th century, Chinese Australian merchants in Sydney established profitable wholesale businesses, importing and exporting produce between both countries. In 1900, an enterprising young merchant, Ma Ying Piu, who was a founding partner of Wing Sang grocery stores in Sydney, opened the first Sincere department store in Hong Kong. In 1912, he expanded to Canton, and in 1917 to Shanghai. He was inspired by the Sydney department stores of the 1890s, Anthony Horderns and Sons and David Jones. In 1907, the two Kwok brothers, Philip Kwok Chin and James Kwok Lock, opened the Wing On department store in Hong Kong. In 1918, they expanded to Shanghai.

Chinese influence and folklore remain with us to this day in little known and appreciated ways. During the Australian goldrush in the mid-1800s, many Chinese workers, mainly from Guangdong Province, went to work in the goldfields to seek their fortune. It is from this time that the slang term *fair dinkum* entered the Australian vernacular: it means that something or someone is real, genuine or authentic. It is thought that this common Australian expression is a derivation of the Cantonese word *ding kum* as in real gold. In Mandarin, it is *ding jin*. But as we have learnt, there is more than gold to Australia's historic links with China. *The Forgotten* is an important and untold chapter in our history which highlights the bonds between our two countries.

After the disasters of Verdun (February 1916) and the Battle of the Somme (July–November 1916), Britain and France sought the assistance of China to send troops to continental Europe to help fight the Germans. Initially China refrained: it had declared itself neutral and did not formally take sides in the First World War until 1917.

But to assist the allies with their war effort, China did send around 145,000 Chinese labourers known as the Chinese Labour Corps (CLC) plus unknown thousands to Russia. The CLC worked behind the lines, digging trenches, laying rail lines, treating the wounded, helping move munitions. At the end of the war, the CLC stayed behind and helped clean up the mess; they buried the dead, they removed barbed wire and unexploded munitions.

British-French estimates put the casualties from 3,000–5,000, but some estimates put this as high as 20,000 CLC. They died from sickness, starvation, diseases, the casualties of war. As they were not military personnel, most were just buried where they fell. Some were laid to rest in the large Chinese cemetery at Noyelles-sur-Mer and on the edge or by the boundary wall of military cemeteries. Their graves are still tended by the Commonwealth War Graves Commission.

As they were poorly paid (they received just one

franc per day), many wanted to stay after the war. But Britain would not allow it and the CLC was forced to return home. France was generous. It allowed an estimated 7,000 CLC men to remain, men who became the genesis of the Chinese population in Europe today.

Back in Australia, some 416,809 young men enlisted for the war. About 330,000 went overseas where one in three was killed or wounded: 60,000 dead and 166,811 wounded. It is through these men that the Australian character of mateship was forged through the ravages of war.

The Australians soon realised that they differed from the British as the British differed from them. We Australians have developed our character through sheer determination, will and true grit. Despite our small population, in international sports or business we often punch well above our weight. Many Australians of Chinese heritage also enrolled to join the fight for their adopted country, but most were turned down. They did not meet the requirement of being of substantial European origin or descent.

In the Second World War, some Chinese Anzacs from the First World War re-enlisted. They served in non-combatant capacities, amongst them, the Shang brothers, Harry Hoyling, Albert Lagoon, Julian Ping, Thomas See, William See and brothers Samuel and

Hedley Tongway. The children and families of Chinese Anzacs who served in the Second World War include the Gum family from South Australia, the Langtips and the Lepps from Victoria and the Shanhuns from Western Australia.

I wish to especially mention certain families. The Chucks family from South Australia had five men serving in the Second Australian Imperial Force. The Mahlook family had 20 family members, 19 men and one woman, serve in the armed forces. Descendants of Kwong Sue Duk, a notable herbalist, had eight grandsons, one granddaughter and five grandsons-in-law who all served. Finally, five members of the family of Major General Darryl Low Choy all served in the Second AIF.

At the declaration of the Second World War, many commercial Chinese seamen were stranded in Australia, unable to return home. With an awareness of the Sino-Japanese War and Japan as a common enemy, over 400 men enlisted in the Second AIF's 7th Employment Company formed as a Chinese-only unit. These men were stationed in Darwin, Townsville and Broome. They served in critical non-combatant roles: they loaded merchant ships, built small sailing craft and grew food for the armed forces.

Australians and Chinese have always been

united. Prior to the ending of the Second World War with the bombs on Hiroshima and Nagasaki, China was the main opponent in curtailing the Japanese advance in the Northern Pacific. It is well recognised that Japanese submarines entered Sydney Harbour, and that Japanese planes bombed Darwin. But Chinese seamen and merchants, stranded in Australia, helped fight the enemy side-by-side with both Australian and Chinese Australian diggers alike.

Many lives were lost, but China as a nation made the greatest sacrifice. Fourteen million Chinese lives were lost in curtailing Japanese aggression. What kind of country might Australia be today were it not for China's efforts in holding back Japan's advance?

How much is known today by the younger generation of the sacrifice made, and the bonds of friendship forged between our countries? Like any relationship, ours has its ups and downs, but we have a shared history. The roots of our friendship run deep. No relationship is stronger than those which involve sacrifice: both sides have sacrificed much. In the interests of both our countries, the story of the Forgotten (CLC and the Chinese Australian Anzacs) needs to be told and shared.

In my earlier comments, I mentioned media reports of Chinese influence in Australia. Given that a little over 5% of the Australian population is of Chinese ethnicity and that it is expected to grow, consider how the Australian palate has evolved over recent decades. Ginger and chili are common Asian ingredients in most Australian homes and restaurants. Nowhere else in the western world would you find a country where the population at large is so adept at using chopsticks. As time goes on, Chinese influence in Australia will strengthen: the mateship between both countries will grow.

Our commercial interests stand on a solid foundation based on a long history of friendship and common interests. Chinese Australians too have had their share of influence on China. Australia is and will continue to be a great friend of China, and maintain our alliance and friendship with the United States. Together, we can all prosper in a peaceful world, but this can only happen provided we do not forget the past. We must always say: 'Lest We Forget'.

For more information on how actions by Australians have benefited China in other ways, please watch the documentary by Sandra Pires: *The Dalfram Dispute 1938*.

Please visit this link to learn about the largest painting on the First World War: *Panthéon de la Guerre*. The efforts of the Chinese Labour Corp and other participants were painted out: *https://www.youtube.com/watch?v=voTiktcgiaE*

Further information is available at: *https://www.theguardian.com/world/2014/aug/14/first-world-war-forgotten-chinese-labour-corps-memorial.*

ACKNOWLEDGEMENTS

I wish to express my sincere thanks to Dr Will Davies. It was he who initially brought the plight of the CLC to my attention.

I would like to thank these institutions and individuals. All of you have supported and encouraged me in this endeavour: the Governor of NSW, His Excellency General the Honourable David Hurley AC DSC (Ret'd); David Gonski AC; Nicholas Moore; Maurice Newman AC; the Hon. Dr Brendan Nelson AO; Paul Monk; Miranda Devine; Michael Smith; Peter Hack; the French Consul-General, Nicolas Crozier; the British Consul-General, Michael Ward; John Mullen; Alan Joyce AC; Geoff Raby; Si Yuan; the Chinese Museum in Melbourne with special thanks to Dr Edmond Chiu AM, Joyce Agee, Dr Sophie Couchman, Emily Cheah Ah-Qune and the volunteer staff; Andrew Forrest AO; the Hon. Peter Dutton; Madam Fu Ying; Dr Yeqin Zuo; El Naismith; Lee Kernaghan; Noel Whittaker; John Van Der Wielen; Nick Farr-Jones AM; Peter Tyree; Sandra Pires; Alan Jones AO; Rhondda Vanzella OAM; Marie Gittard; Caroline Terode; Jo Olsen; Heather Davies; the Hon. Warwick Smith AO; Tom Seymour; Barry Shying; Jeff McMullen; Rob Macklin;

the Hon. David Elliott; the Hon. Bob Carr; the Hon. Anthony Roberts; Nathaniel Smith; Peter Anstee; Malcolm Turnbull and Premier Gladys Berejiklian. Our editors, Helena Bond and Benjamin Taaffe, our publisher, Michael Wilkinson and Jess Lomas of Wilkinson Publishing, and publicist Max Markson.

If I have inadvertently left anyone out, please forgive me.

Finally, I wish to thank my late father, Dr Kai-Fou Wong whom I miss dearly. He always inspired my brothers and me to strive to do our best at whatever we do. I thank my dear mother, Mrs Kaye Wong, for her cautious encouragement.

Lastly, I thank my dearest wife Sophie and my children Courtney and Taylor for their constant support and inspiration for me to better myself throughout this journey of discovery and our mission to share this knowledge with all.

May God bless Australia and all who live here!

REFERENCES

Clyne, J & others *Chinese Anzacs*, Department of Veterans Affairs, Chinese Museum and History Teachers Association of Victoria, Canberra 2015

Fitzgerald, S. *Red Tape, Gold Scissors: the story of Sydney's Chinese*, State Library of NSW Press for the City of Sydney, 1997

Hack, P.J. *The Art Deco Department Stores of Shanghai,* Impact Press, Sydney 2017

Hamilton, J. *Gallipoli Sniper: The Life of Billy Sing* Pan McMillan, Sydney, 2009

Loh, M. *Dinki-di: The contributions of Chinese Immigrants and Australians of Chinese Descent to Australia's Defence Forces and War Efforts, 1899-1988*, Australian Government Publishing Service, Canberra 1989

Macklin, R. *Dragon and Kangaroo* Hachette Australia, Sydney, 2017

O'Neill, M. *The Chinese Labour Corps*, Penguin, Melbourne 2014.

Poon, H. *Two Sides of the Coin: The True Life Story of an Australian Born Chinaman*, Self-published, 1996

Xu Guoqi. *Strangers on the Western Front: Chinese Workers in the Great War*, Harvard University Press, Cambridge Mass, 2011

Nine masted junk of Admiral Zheng. Columbus's *La Pinta* beside to show scale.

郑和率领的九桅帆船。旁边是哥伦比亚率领的拉平塔船以示比较。

Elizabeth Farm, Sydney.

帕拉马塔伊丽莎白农场.

John Blaxland.

约翰·布莱克斯兰 .

Early Macau – British East India Company.

早年的澳门 – 英国东印度公司.

The popular English tea party.

受欢迎的英国式茶会.

The Chinese navy were no match to the European navies they came up against.

中国海军不是欧洲海军的对手.

A contemporary depiction of an action in the Taiping Rebellion.

当时对太平天国起义的描绘.

A cartoon depicting the slicing up of China by the European powers.

一张描绘欧洲列强瓜分中国的漫画.

John Macarthur.

约翰・麦克阿瑟.

The port of Macau.

19世纪70年代的澳门港.

Convicts in old Sydney town. (1830).

在老悉尼城的罪犯.

The expanding colony of Sydney.

不断扩大的悉尼殖民地.

Chinese work a sluice on the Californian goldfields.

中国人在加州的金矿区.

Chinese labourers laying a railway line in the western USA.

中国劳工在美国西部铺铁路.

A Chinese store on the Victorian goldfields.

维多利亚金矿区的一家中国商店.

A cartoon from the Lambing Flats riots.

一张有关产羔牧场暴乱的漫画.

The Empress Dowager being carried on a litter.
慈禧太后坐在轿子上.

Commodore Matthew Perry.
马修·佩里准将.

A contemporary cartoon depicting the Chinese octopus.
当时一张描绘中国八爪鱼的漫画（见细节）.

Australian journalist George Morrison in China.
澳大利亚记者乔治·莫里森在中国.

Australian journalist William Donald with the nationalist leader Chang Hsueh-Liang.
澳大利亚记者威廉　唐纳德与国民党领导人张学良.

Japanese lithograph of their new navy.
有关日本海军的日本石版画.

Chinese 'Boxers' fighters.
义和团团员.

Defending the European embassies in the Peking siege.
在北京解围战中保护欧洲使馆.

Emperor Guangxu.
光绪皇帝.

The wives of European diplomats are entertained for tea by the Empress Dowager Cixi.
慈禧太后茶会招待欧洲外交官的妻子.

Sun Yat-sen.
孙中山/孙逸仙.

Emperor Piyi aged two years.
两岁的溥仪皇帝.

General Yuan Shikai.
袁世凯大元帅.

German battleship at Tsingtao.
德国战列舰在青岛.

ning World. WAR EXTRA!
"Circulation Books Open to All."
DAY, AUGUST 1, 1914. 10 PAGES PRICE ONE CENT.
CLARES WAR;
E IS IN ARMS
sador, in the name of his Government, sent to the Rus-
laration of war.
urg telegraph agency, which is considered the official
ITALY BREAKS THE TRIPLE ALLIANCE;
FRANCE CALLS OUT HER WAR ARMY
7,474,000 ANSWER FIRST CALL; 7 WARRING NATIONS CAN PUT 32,541,000 MEN IN THE FIELD
England Gives Formal Notice That She Will Side With France and Russia and Back Up Her Agreements to the Full Extent of Her Power and Resources.

Declaration of war, 1914
1914年人们是如何得知宣战的. 的.

German cruisers of the Far East Squadron at Tsingsao.
在青岛的德国远东中队的巡洋舰.

Wreck of SMS *Emden*, Cocos Island, after the engagement with HMAS *Sydney*.
在科科斯群岛与悉尼号作战后的埃姆登号残骸.

Liang Shiyi.
梁士诒.

French troops during the Battle of the Marne, late 1914.
法国军队在马恩河战役，1914年下半年.

Australian volunteers in late 1914.
1914年下半年澳大利亚自愿者.

Private William "Billy" Sing DCM
一等兵威廉·“比利”·辛殊功勋章.

Billy Sing in his snipers post at Gallipoli.
比利 辛在加里波利的阻击手岗位.

Chinese men of the Chinese Labour Corp prepare to board a ship for overseas service.

中国劳工旅的人准备乘船去海外服务.

Chinese Labour Corp men at the front.

中国劳工旅的人在前线.

Chinese Labour Corp men in front of their Nissan hut.

中国劳工旅的人在尼森式铁皮屋前.

Chinese Labour Corp men working, loading and storing ammunition in massive dumps behind the frontline.

中国劳工在前线附近装卸和储存弹药.

Australian machine gunners returning from the front line, Pozieres August 1916.

1916年8月波济耶尔战役中澳大利亚机枪手离开火线.

The mud encountered by the advancing Australians in the fighting towards Passchendaele, late 1917.

1917年年尾澳大利亚士兵在战斗中向帕斯耶尔进攻的路上碰到的泥泞.

The village of Dernancourt today - the battlefield of 1918.

现在的德南库尔村和1918年的战场.

Caleb Shang DCM & Bar, MM.

卡勒布・达可布　尚，获殊功勋章.

Sidney Shang.

西德尼・伍　尚.

Henry Langtip.
亨利·兰蒂普.

Leslie Langtip.
莱斯利·兰蒂普.

Bertie Langtip.
伯迪·兰蒂普.

Unknown Australian gravestone.
在法国的一个不知名的
澳大利亚士兵的墓.

The Empress of Russia converted and camouflaged for war.

俄罗斯女皇号.

Members of the Chinese Labour Corps at a railway yard with three unidentified staff of the 2nd Australian Light Railway Operating Company.

中国劳工旅劳工在一个铁路车场与澳大利亚第二轻铁工程连的三名成员合影.

Chinese Labour Corp workers stacking shells in a dump behind the frontline.

劳工旅将炮弹堆放在战线后的存放处.

Chinese Labour Corp workers employed in a range of jobs including factory work and maintaining tanks.

中国人受雇于一系列工作.

Chinese Labour Corp workers doing mechanical repairs.

中国劳工旅劳工在做机械修理工作.

German prisoners captured by Australians after their advance in August 1918.

一九一八年八月攻击战后澳军抓获的德军俘虏.

Sinking of the *ATHOS*.

法国客船阿索斯号沉没.

Gates of the Chinese Cemetery at Noyelles-sur-Mer and headstones.
海滨诺埃尔中国公墓的大门, 公墓里的墓.

Men of the CLC on board a train in Canada on their return journey to Vancouver.

归途中中国劳工旅的人在加拿大将要上火车前往温哥华。

Wellington Koo. 顾维钧.

Codford AIF camp on the Salisbury Plain in England where men waited for a ship home.

Billy Sing and his wife Elizabeth Stewart.
比利・辛和他的妻子伊丽莎白・斯图尔特.

Chinese Labour Corp were employed in a range of jobs including maintaining tanks.

包括工厂工作和坦克维修.

Family members on the wharf awaiting Caleb Shang's return home.

卡勒布·尚的家人在码头等待他的荣归。

A small section of the massive painting 'Pantheon de la Guerre'.

巨幅画“战争的万神殿”的一个小部分

The smiling face of men of the Chinese Labour Corps.

中国劳工旅劳工的笑脸.

被遗忘的人们

第一次世界大战中的中国劳工旅及澳纽军团的华人将士

维尔·戴维斯博士（澳大利亚国立大学）著

前言 布兰登·纳尔逊医生 官佐勋位

序言 阿尔伯特·黄汝宁先生 员佐勋位

出版发行：
Wilkinson Publishing Pty Ltd
ACN 006 042 173
Level 4, 2 Collins St Melbourne, Victoria, Australia 3000
Ph: +61 3 9654 5446
www.wilkinsonpublishing.com.au

A catalogue record for this book is available from the National Library of Australia

计划出版日期：02-2020
书名：被遗忘的人们 — 第一次世界大战中的中国劳工旅及澳纽 军团的华人将士
ISBN(s)：9781925927238：印刷 — 平装本

本书的目录记录可从
澳大利亚国家图书馆查找。

封面艺术：方力钧2016年作品丝绸木刻版画，
12版，244厘米x 366厘米，由方力钧和朱雀艺术提供，
网址vermilionart.com.au。
澳纽军团插图：爱伦 奈斯米斯。
中文翻译：钱彦.

印刷装帧：澳大利亚理格乐有限公司

封底感言

过去四年来，我们回顾了澳纽军团在第一次世界大战中的贡献，又发现了许多新故事。正是由于阿尔伯特・黄（Albert Wong）的执着追求和维尔・戴维斯（Will Davies）的细心发掘，这个鲜为人知的故事让我们了解到人们曾经为战争、特别是为澳纽军团做出的贡献。中国劳工旅为前线提供物资补给和人员支持，在这方面为盟军作战出力。这个故事还揭示了众多华人在服役于澳大利亚皇家军队期间的壮举。这是一个值得讲述的故事，内容有关对于澳纽军团的奉献和支持，给人留下了深刻印象。

澳大利亚联邦总督大卫・赫尔利
（David Hurley AC DSC）将军阁下

百年纪念活动的重大意义之一就是有机会讲述那些此前被遗忘的故事，让我们深入了解多元文化和英雄主义。恭喜威尔・戴维斯（Will Davies）挖掘出了其中的一些故事。

新南威尔士州议会反恐怖主义部部长、惩教部
部长暨退伍军人事务部部长
大卫・艾略特（David Elliott）

这本书籍的及时出版提醒我们，不要忘记华人在这次大战中对澳纽军团的贡献以及在这场战争中对盟国的支援。这也告诉大家，中国以及中国人民与我们国家之间拥有长久而牢固的友谊基础。

新南威尔士大学名誉校长大卫・贡斯基
（David Gonski AC）

《被遗忘的人们》贡献了具有启发性的分析，帮助我们了解尚在起步阶段的澳大利亚和陷入困境的中国在那个战乱年代的早期关系。澳大利亚一直是一个移民国家，早期的华人移民在塑造我们的社会方面发挥了重要作用。在这本书中，维尔・戴维斯（Will Davies）博士阐明了中国在一战期间为盟军所作的、但经常被忽视的实质性贡献。这些章节讲述了我们历

史上激动人心的一页，展示了澳纽军团的传奇如何影响我们这个多元文化社会的各个角落。我们决不能忘记，为了捍卫澳大利亚价值观和建立这个自由繁荣的国度，我们曾肩并肩付出了多少牺牲。

内政部部长、移民和边境保护部部长
彼得·达顿（Peter Dutton）议员

这本书概述了第一次世界大战期间20万中国工人在支持盟军方面鲜为人知的贡献，以及在战争期间澳大利亚华人参军的功绩。感谢维尔·戴维斯（Will Davies）和阿尔伯特·黄（Albert Wong）为《被遗忘的人们》所做的重要工作和关键贡献。感谢您分享这个故事，它勾画了我们丰富而多样的历史，并将使后代的澳大利亚人受益。

新南威尔士州议会残疾人服务
部部长、多元文化部部长
雷·威廉姆斯（Ray Williams）议员

由阿尔伯特·黄（Albert Wong）委托维尔·戴维斯（Will Davies）推出这本书籍，着重介绍了为一战和二战做出贡献却“被遗忘”的中国人和澳大利亚华人。作为位于墨尔本的澳大利亚华人历史博物馆（华人博物馆），我们很高兴看到这样的合作，有望使澳大利亚人认识到中国人和澳大利亚华人曾经的付出、苦难和牺牲，也令今世后代的澳大利亚人铭记于心。让我们永志不忘。

墨尔本华人博物馆志愿研究员埃德蒙·邱
（Edmond Chiu AM）博士

被遗忘的澳纽军团是世界历史的重要组成部分，这也是对亚太国家共同命运的重要提醒。阿尔伯特·黄（Albert Wong）和维尔·戴维斯（Will Davies）值得赞扬，他们将这段历史拂去尘埃，并以长期被遗忘的战争英雄和华裔军人在多场激烈战事中的壮举作为叙事对象。

这项至关重要的研究为中国和澳大利亚的共

同历史开辟了新的视角，也很好地回顾了两国在上个世纪为促进我们地区和平所作的共同努力。

福特斯库金属集团创始人兼董事长、慈善家
安德鲁·福雷斯特（Andrew Forrest AO）

《被遗忘的人们》是一本特别的书，它仿佛一束光，照亮了那些鲜为人知的历史情节。这也提醒了我们，对于过去的重要史实和自己的国家民族居然所知甚少。维尔·戴维斯（Will Davies）详细地叙述了在中国秘密招募的中国劳工旅（CLC）如何在西线支援包括华裔澳纽军团在内的盟军。在书写这段被遗忘的历史时，戴维斯不仅使我们想起了中国劳工旅为支持身处前线的华裔澳纽军团而做出的重要贡献，也使我们意识到华裔为澳大利亚做出了更广泛的贡献，却在很大程度上未获认可。本书出版的时机也很重要，目前澳大利亚正在努力适应中国的迅速崛起及其世界强国的地位，而华裔背景也已占到澳大利亚人口的5%以上。他们现在可以愉快地回顾澳纽军团的这部分传统。阿尔伯特·黄（Albert Wong）对于该项目的大力支持值得特别称赞。

2007-2011年前澳大利亚驻华大使杰夫·拉比
（Geoff Raby）

被遗忘的人们》是在重要时期出版的非凡著作。今年是第一次世界大战结束一百周年，同时有关中国影响力的辩论也已经转向民族主义方向，比如有澳大利亚华裔公民被指控为中国共产党的阴谋共犯。《被遗忘的人们》记载了澳大利亚华人在一战中为我们国家付出的牺牲和表现的英雄主义，都属于我们国家的历史传奇，却鲜少有人传颂这些伟大贡献。本书详细介绍了许多澳大利亚华人加入澳纽军团后的英勇事迹，例如比利·辛（Billy Sing）、卡勒布（Caleb）、西德尼·尚（Sidney Shang）和朗蒂普（Langtip）兄弟，以及中国劳工旅在战时支持英法盟军所取得的历史性功绩。而在此过程中，他们还遭受了各种苦难、种族主义和排斥忽视的待遇。这本书的内容提醒我们，澳大利亚和中国曾经为了反抗独裁暴政而并肩作战，澳

大利亚华人一直都是我们的一员，从非原住民移居澳大利亚的发展早期就开始建设和捍卫我们的国家，因而澳大利亚华人和任何其他澳大利亚人一样，都归属于这个国家，也都值得信任。

悉尼大学参议会成员李逸仙（Jason Yat-sen Li）

回顾历史的各个方面是大有裨益的，何况这是澳纽军团和一战的历史，对于澳大利亚和我们的民族国家意识都至关重要。但这对于我们国家中的少数群体而言更为重要，例如华人。他们在1850年代饱受歧视，却在德国及其盟军威胁到大英帝国成员国——澳大利亚时，以行动证明了自己对这个新家园的忠诚。当我们回顾这片移民国土之上的人口迁移时，确实需要诉说《被遗忘的人们》这个故事。

1996澳大利亚年度人物余森美（John Yu）

被遗忘的人们》可谓一个重要的提醒，即了解我们的历史对建设澳大利亚未来至关重要。莫纳什将军本人在对战争的总结中写道，法国的巨大胜利来自于“所有人”的贡献。这本书使我们意识到，为了获得成功，整个国家团结一致有多么重要

约翰·莫纳什爵士奖学金基金会主席吉莲·西格尔（Jillian Segal AO）

维尔·戴维斯（Will Davies）收集了一些绝佳资料，向在第一次世界大战期间为澳大利亚军队服务却“被遗忘”的中国人致以敬意和认可。这些中国公民赶赴一战战场，在战争期间不懈工作，为盟军提供了多项服务。战后，其中许多人留在法国，形成了巴黎华人社区的核心。戴维斯的文笔将战争宏观背景、欧洲内部影响与华人劳工的事迹结合在一起。人们不应忘记在那场战争中人们为争取自由所付出的牺牲，并且中国人民的奉献和参与也为战争结局发挥了至关重要的作用，值得全世界的感谢。

澳大利亚资本投资有限公司委员主席
沃里克·史密斯（Warwick Smith AO）阁下

他们是政府政策下的种族主义受害者。在白澳年代，他们被视作外人。但是，无论是参加澳纽军团还是进入华人劳工旅，他们都为自己的国家而服务奉献，毫不犹豫。简而言之，他们曾与澳大利亚站在一起。这也是历史留给今天的一条讯息：澳大利亚华人是良好的公民，我们应保护其免受白澳政策所遗留的无端怀疑，摒弃对其不忠于澳大利亚的阴险指控。

新南威尔士州任职时间最长的总理、
澳大利亚前外交部部长
鲍勃·卡尔（Bob Carr）阁下

通过深刻而细致的工作，维尔·戴维斯（Will Davies）博士和阿尔伯特·黄（Albert Wong）为这一段历史提供了新的启示。除了历史事实，这本书也是对一战中被遗忘的人们致敬，使我们想起了我们各国由于共同的历史遭遇而建立的紧密联系。

法国驻悉尼总领事尼古拉斯·克罗泽
（Nicolas Croizer）

感谢阿尔伯特·黄（Albert Wong）和维尔·戴维斯（Will Davies）的绝佳叙事，使我和许多其他人都能了解到中国劳工旅在一战中支持澳新军团及盟军而表现的勇气和牺牲。戴维斯在历史宏观背景下，对于许多中国人及其家庭的英雄主义和苦难经历展开了令人信服的个体描述。希望通过阿尔伯特·黄的委托和威尔·戴维斯的学术，这些被遗忘的澳纽军团成员不会再次被遗忘。也希望这本书能有助于大家更全面地理解这段由重大冲突事件写就的多元且复杂的文化历史，因为也是这些塑造了如今的世界和我们辉煌的多样化社会。

英国驻悉尼总领事迈克尔·沃德（Michael Ward）

目录

前言

澳大利亚国家战争纪念馆馆长布兰登·纳尔逊 官佐勋位

中国劳工旅由约二十万来自农村的中国劳工组成。第一次世界大战中他们在异常艰苦且极为危险的条件下在西线战场为英法军工作，有两万人死于战场。尽管在战争中做出如此大的贡献，他们中的大多数人在战后却被赶出境。他们的故事常常遭到忽略。

对中国当局来说，中国劳工旅代表不需要直接军事承诺的情况下为战争努力作贡献的一种方式。对法国和英国来说，这些人成为在前线被剥削的劳动力，为盟军的集体战争行动增添了关键的人力。

此书将中国劳工旅的故事放在1700年以来中国与西欧国家交往的更广泛的历史之中来看。另外，同时期还有大量的中国人移民来到澳大利亚，也是这段历史的一部分。正是这些华人定居者的儿子、孙子和重孙们在第一次世界大战中自愿奋起为澳大利亚战斗。这些人是澳纽军团华人将士。

在澳大利亚国家战争纪念馆的阵亡将士名册上列出了因为参战而死亡的十万两千多澳大利亚男人与女人。在这些当中有列兵亚瑟·威廉·莫的名字，他第一次世界大战中在第三十九营服役。他出生在维多利亚西部斯多沃尔，父亲叫阿莫，是中国人，母亲叫玛丽，是英国人。亚瑟的两个兄弟查理和约翰也在澳大利亚帝国军服役。三人都参加了1917年6月在比利时的梅西纳大战。亚瑟在战斗中受伤，数小时内便死于战伤。他的两个兄弟活过了战争。

亚瑟·莫是第一次世界大战中在澳大利亚帝国军中服役的两百多名华裔澳大利亚人之一。其中四十多名为他们所选为家园的国家做出了最终的牺牲，然而

这个国家却并非总是欢迎他们的祖先的。

在十九世纪的澳大利亚殖民地，中国人作矿工、菜农、和商人。Lowe Kong Meng（刘光明）便是这样一个商人，他是维多利亚州最富有的商人之一。他的两个儿子自愿为他们所出生的国家参战。这两兄弟所走过的道路将在本书后面详细叙述。哥哥在西线战场打仗，弟弟两次被拒入伍，原因是欧洲血统不足。华人后裔要求服役常常会面对这种额外的障碍，但如这个例子所示，规则的使用并不总是不变的。

尽管华人定居者在十九世纪的澳大利亚是不受欢迎的，但1914年英国和德国之间爆发战争时，很多华裔澳大利亚人奋起保卫他们的国土家园。有些一直战斗到战争快结束，却在最后的几个星期里丧失了生命。朗塞斯顿人列兵纳尔逊·辛在1918年10月3日法国蒙布勒安附近一战中澳大利亚步兵的最后一次战役中阵亡。

澳纽军团华裔将士与欧洲、土著和其他民族背景的将士并肩奋战，也在战友中得到了接纳：在兄弟同伴之间是没有歧视的。

来自中国人移民到澳大利亚已有两个世纪，自由定居者麦世英1818年就到澳大利亚。从那时开始，华裔澳大利亚人参与了国家所有的决定性事件。十九世纪时在有些地方他们遭到来自欧洲背景的澳大利亚人的种族歧视甚至身体虐待，立法者还特别针对他们制定歧视性立法。尽管如此，华裔背景的澳大利亚人为澳大利亚历史做出了丰厚的贡献。

作为现代历史的一部分，中国劳工旅和澳纽军团华人将士的故事是对他们在战争中的贡献表示敬意。本书向公众讲述了一个重要的故事。

序言

黄汝宁先生 员佐勋位

为了所有那些付出一切的人，为了对国家的热爱，为了对我们的后人的热爱。

我请维尔·戴维斯博士写这本书的灵感来自一次通过共同的朋友澳大利亚橄榄球传奇人物 尼克·法尔·琼斯的介绍偶然与他相识。维尔在带领参观战场时看到西线战场上有中国劳工的坟墓。他化了相当长的时间寻求支持和承认他称之为’被遗忘的人们’，约二十万名中国劳工（简称CLC - 中国劳工旅），主要是从中国山东派去协助同盟国跟随前线挖战壕、修铁路和埋葬倒下的战士。据信，到战争结束的时候，约两万中国劳工死于疾病、饥饿以及战火造成的附带伤害。付给他们的报酬极低，很多人没有足够的资金回家。战后法国允许一些人留下，这些人成为欧洲华人社区的种子。但大多数人不允许留下。即使在1918年停战协定签订以后他们帮助清理了战场，最终他们还是被遣返回国。他们掩埋了尸体、抬运了伤者，排除了未爆的炸弹。

在调研中，我们还发现了一个鲜为人知的事实，即在澳大利亚帝国军中有数百名华人澳大利亚一战士兵。他们是澳纽军团华裔将士，特别是得到勋章的凯勒布·尚（Caleb Shang），和加里波利狙击手沈比利(Billy Sing)。当然这都是过去的事，为什么现在要旧事重提呢？象生活中的很多事情一样，我相信时机与命运。我并没有去故意寻找这些，是维尔来找到了我，是他将中国劳工的困境引起了我的注意。我在澳大利亚生活了四十三年：这儿是我的家，我的根在这儿。然而直到现在，每次澳纽军团日时我虽然认识到这是一个神圣的日子，但以前总是感到是个局外人。我没有参加过纪念活动，然而我心里总是很感激那些

为澳大利亚，为维护和保护我们的传统和价值、我们的自由和我们的生活方式做出最大牺牲的人。我希望共享那种澳大利亚的同属感。我坚信必须保护我们的价值观和生活方式。我不希望看到我们的澳大利亚价值受到侵蚀。为了对得起那些牺牲自己生命的人，我们要保护我们的生活方式。

我希望这本书被写的目的有二。首先是认识过去和澄清过去。同时也是确保年轻的澳大利亚人以及特别是未来的世世代代了解中国人在第一次世界大战中的参与，了解中国人以及包括印度劳工旅、斐济劳工旅和埃及劳工旅等其他族裔群所做的牺牲。

我们是一个多种族的社会，有多元混合的丰富文化。我们也都是澳大利亚人，我们为了自己应该确保澳大利亚的公平、包容、兄弟情谊的文化得到保存和传承。无论是华裔还是其他族裔，新移民群体都必须接收澳大利亚的文化及其价值观。澳大利亚人口的百分之五以上现在是华人，中国是澳大利亚的重要贸易伙伴和朋友。象所有的良好的友谊一样，我们两个文化可以有不同意见和误解。但是好朋友应该能够超越过去的不同意见，珍惜我们共有的东西，这既在人口的混合方面，也在共享的历史方面。

我真诚地希望澳大利亚与中国之间有益、紧密的联系将继续增长和巩固。也许有一天澳大利亚人会熟练地说中文，就象他们现在很会使用筷子一样。

导言

二十多年来我在西线战场上漫游徘徊的时候，发现了中国劳工旅的坟墓。他们常常被掩映在英联邦战争墓地的角落，与其他坟墓分开，常常沿着篱笆或隔墙。很少有人来看望：他们是被遗忘的人。

这引起我的好奇：他们是谁？我做了点调研，发现了他们被派遣和服役的故事。我想谁知道这些人们。他们安息在远离家乡和亲人的地方，在遥远的中国谁关心这些被遗忘的中国劳工？

这些被遗忘的人需要被记住。我开始的时候是希望从悉尼的华人社区寻求一笔很小的捐助（我的估计是大约五千澳元），然后也许在中国城或更好是在中国花园的围墙里竖一块铜匾以示纪念。四年没有结果后我放弃了。

后来我的老朋友彼得·泰理和尼克·法尔·琼斯介绍我认识了阿尔伯特˙黄汝宁先生。我给他讲了我称之为’被遗忘的人们’ 的故事。他立即被这段鲜为人知的历史所吸引，当他晚上告诉他的母亲时，他母亲也被吸引。如阿尔伯特所说：’我从无知到着魔’。这使他不仅想为这些人竖一块纪念碑，而且要委托我写一本书，一本澳大利亚年轻人容易读懂，特别是澳大利亚华人以及他们的移民父母容易读懂的书。

本书便是其结果。在我做调研的过程中，特别是在埃德蒙邱博士以及墨尔本中国博物馆员工的帮助下，我还了解到澳纽军团的华人将士的故事。这也成为广泛的故事的一部分。我在这方面的希望是澳大利亚华人能认识到他们也是澳大利亚澳纽军团传统的一部分，中国血统的澳大利亚人为了他们的这个国家战斗和流血牺牲。如阿尔巴特说：’我以前从来没有参

加过澳纽军团纪念日的纪念活动或游行，但是现在我觉得自己是这个传统的一部分，是这一重要的纪念场合的一部分。’

希望您喜欢这个故事。希望您象阿尔伯特一样，会觉得自己是澳纽军团纪念传统的一部分，会体会到它在澳大利亚社会中的地位。

第一章 两百年以前

2018年澳大利亚纪念了第一位到澳大利亚定居的中国人，一位在1818年跳船上岸的水手。虽然有些人声称中国航海家郑和约1421年带领他的庞大的九桅帆木船船队到过澳大利亚，比库克船长要早350年，但这种说法至今未得到证实，并且仍然是颇有争议的。

但是这位中国定居者是真实的：他的名字叫麦世英（Mak Sai Ying）。他于1818年2月27日乘劳蕾尔号船到悉尼下船，是自由定居者， 第一舰队到达后刚刚30年，悉尼当时仍是一个艰苦、饥饿和偏远的定居地。

对于罪犯而言，生活特别艰难，但是对于中国海员来说呢？ 由于他有限的英语和亚洲人的脸孔，他会受到孤立并当作受排斥者来对待。但是他拥有当时短缺的技能：他是木匠和橱柜制造匠。

麦世英于1789年出生于广州。在广州这个重要的贸易港口，他可能与英国的交易商和贸易商有过接触。象后来黄金潮时期来到澳大利亚的很多中国人一样，以前几乎没有接触过圆眼睛、黄色、红色或沙色的头发、白皮肤的欧洲人。

也许因为他的技能，麦世英在两个拥有土地的大家庭找到了工作。起先他在约翰·布莱克斯兰的纽因顿庄园工作，他与约翰·布莱克斯兰是在劳蕾尔号船上认识的，毫无疑问建立了友谊。事实上约翰·布莱克斯兰很尊重麦世英，他付给他的工资与给自由的英国雇员一样，这在当时是极为不寻常的事。约翰的兄弟格利高里·布莱克斯兰是1813年第一个越过蓝山的人之一。布莱克斯兰家是富有并极受尊敬的社会成员。

有木工技能，又有人推荐，麦世英还在麦克阿瑟家找到了工作，。麦克阿瑟家拥有大片的牧场，特别是在

帕拉马塔和卡姆登周围。

到澳大利亚以后，麦世英将自己的名字英语化成为约翰·施英（John Shying）。到1820年，他开始在帕拉马塔的伊丽莎白农场工作，还有另外两个中国人：一个厨师和一个家庭佣人。约翰·麦克阿瑟发现他的中国工人可靠、勤劳、节俭，有值得称赞的品质，而以往用的是不守规则的罪犯。他觉得，在这些人身上也许有一个新的和有利可图的生意，但他必须尽早介入。

中国移民并非新的观念。当年随库克船长来的詹姆斯·马特勒（他的名字仍在东悉尼的马特勒维尔区中长存），计划在新荷兰建立一个罪犯流放地的时候曾建议一项中国移民的项目，以满足可能短缺技术工匠的需要。没过多久中国作为一个潜在的市场和可靠有技能的劳动力供应来源就在殖民地的管理者和土地所有人脑子里找到了位置。

第二章 一段悠久的历史

然而，故事远在很早之前就已开始。远在欧洲人到来之前，中国是个很强大和进步的国家，是个政治上统一，人口繁密，受过良好教育，有文化修养，能够养活自己的人民的国家。从欧洲的角度来看，中国不是一个工业的国家，肯定不象工业革命时期的欧洲国家，欧洲国家当时在制造方式、新产品和军事技术方面已走在了世界的前面。

打开这个神秘而古老的土地进行贸易是欧洲贸易商的梦想。虽然在1700年以前对中国的了解很少，但在13世纪后期意大利威尼斯探险家马可·波罗来过这个国家两次，并写下了他的冒险经历。在探险时代，西方的兴趣增加：包括荷兰、法国、西班牙、葡萄牙和英国在内的国家都在中国建立了贸易港口。

随着探险家和贸易商的到来，天主教传教士也来了，特别是方济各会的传教士，他们在14世纪就开始，随后是耶稣教派，他们在中国各地广泛旅行、传教并劝人们皈依基督教。虽然这在中国朝庭引起极大关注，甚至有时禁止他们的传教，但也有些人成为皇帝的亲信和顾问。后来基督教传教士成为暴力的对象：教堂被烧毁，传教士和皈依基督教的中国人都被谋杀。

在17世纪，更多的探险家和贸易商寻求了解中国以及开始与中国开展贸易，但大多数情况下他们的入侵是受到限制的，他们的贸易限于口岸地区。第一个对中国的重大入侵是在澳门建立了一个葡萄牙贸易港口。1711年英国东印度公司也在澳门建立了一个贸易港口，但是中国人的怨恨在增加。

认识到外国人持续不断的入侵，清朝朝廷试图限制贸易的扩展，限制新的外国公司进入市场。当认识到他们无法遏制这些活动时，1760年朝廷引进了一项

通商制度，后来以’一口通商’（Canton System）为人所知。这迫使外国商人不能象以前那样直接与中国人交易，而只能与得到批准的中国商人交易。

通过这种方式，中国得以在19世纪前保持和遏制西方贸易影响。’一口通商’制不仅使中国政府可以限制贸易，而且可以将贸易限制在三个口岸：广东、澳门和香港。来自欧洲交易对手国家的压力最终迫使清朝朝廷放宽制度，19世纪20年代后期，新的欧洲蒸汽船只迫使了港口的开放，将贸易从沿海延伸到中国内地。

在英国，从18世纪中开始茶成为人们最喜爱的饮料，对进口茶叶的需求猛增。中国是一个主要出口国，茶叶可以用来交换如金、银、首饰等欧洲奢侈品。在需要另一个贸易商品的情况下，英国开始从印度进一种使人上瘾的毒品，鸦片。虽然鸦片对中国人来说并非是新事，但现在突然变得可以低价买到，并且可以大量买到。从1729年开始成千上万的鸦片馆兴旺发展，在这些地方，特别是年轻人集聚，陷入吸毒造成的神智恍惚之中。这自然引起清朝朝廷的注意，开始禁止进口鸦片和禁止使用鸦片。

事件发展得很快。首先，中国当局在广州封锁进口鸦片。当英国要求赔偿时，中国拒绝了。这导致了中国当局与英国进口商的冲突，而英国政府在背后积极地支持英国进口商。当一位清朝官员没收了两万箱英国鸦片，约一千两百多吨，并毁了这些鸦片时，英国迅速做出反应，派遣其皇家海军围攻港口，这导致了人们所知道的第一次鸦片战争。

由此导致1842年的《南京条约》。该条约不仅割让包括香港在内的五个中国沿海港口给英国，而且承诺取消’一口通商’制，赔偿战争费用。另外，英国坚持’最惠国待遇’，确保他们在贸易问题上比其他欧洲国家有优先。这对道光皇帝和清朝朝廷是一个很

大的羞辱，对中国的民族自尊和国际声望是个很大的打击，特别是进一步开放了中国对外国通商。

对于中国人来说， 这是一个难以下咽的新教训。他们以前不知道在英国的职业陆海军的军事力量和技术与中国自己的原始武器和战术之间存在巨大差异。这种差异的根源是五十年前1790年乾隆皇帝的固步自封和不明智的政策，后来导致了全国范围内的暴动和叛乱，地方军阀从中央政府夺走了权利。

第三章 可怕的难题

中国现在处于严重的两难境地，一方面要保护传统信念，另一方面要接收西方的改革观念。第一次鸦片战争的灾难不仅仅引起中国大众造反与不满，而且强迫清朝朝廷面对外国的入侵。西方新的管理方式、技术、军事硬件和激进的政治改革，无疑从中国的角度来看，将中国拉入了19世纪和一个崭新的未来。在痛恨外国野蛮人的同时，中国人将注意力转向内部对改革和割让的反应，从而导致进一步的叛乱和衰变。中国认识到必须觉醒过来面对不愉快的变化：一个令人望之生畏并且痛苦的前景。

仿佛这还不够似的，另外两个因素给中国政府和皇帝的脆弱控制施加了进一步压力。首先，中国人口迅速增长。即使有美国的新的农作物和种子，食物还是成为一个关键的问题，这给清朝带来压力。其次，广泛的洪灾加剧了这个问题，政府被怪罪没有给与维持减涝安全措施方面足够的注意。在农村，农民面对作物毁坏食物短缺的情况，同时税务和土地租金在增加。很多人离开地主拿起武器反抗他们认为腐败和邪恶的制度。

这场动乱引发了灾难性的和血腥的太平天国运动，从1850年开始了一段到处混战民间混乱的时期，反映出中国新的民族主义、政治和宗教运动与传统的大清王朝的权力和控制之间的斗争。代表双方的庞大军队发生冲突，伤亡惨重，被任一方俘虏的人通常是被处死。不仅如此，而且在战乱地区，村庄被烧遭劫，平民被杀。

太平天国运动始于广东地区。城市被占时，据信多达一千万的人被杀，这是全面战争：平民和牲畜被杀，农庄被烧，农田被毁。在十四年的战乱中，叛乱蔓延到中国各地很多地方，最终借助于外国军事援助

和领导才平息下去。但是到了叛乱结束时的1864年，估计有两千万至三千万的人死亡，比第一次世界大战军事和平民加起来的总死亡人数还高。

这一毁灭性的叛乱强迫传统中国以及皇帝的权力做出巨大改变。现在中国已被欧洲贸易国瓜分。在中国国内有关如何面对许多各种各样的挑战，有关尤其需要以及进行什么改革开始了迫切的新的讨论。这本身就在中国社会内部造成新的紧张局势，在那些呼吁激烈改革摒弃传统方式的人和那些捍卫传统价值观、文化和皇帝统治的保守派之间的紧张局势。

此时的中国，使情况更糟糕的是，在1856年中国又与英法联军开始了第二次鸦片战争，或英国称作’亚罗号战’。从第一次鸦片战争结束起，欧洲列强便强迫中国扩大市场，并且进入内地寻找更多贸易机会和开放新的贸易港口，使鸦片合法化，以及开放内地。他们还要求允许英国大使在北京建大使馆。

战争的导火线是1854年10月英国船亚罗号因涉嫌是海盗船而被搜索。虽然该船曾被海盗所用，但当时是一条合法的商船。中国水师上船搜索，英国国旗被扯下。这促使英国驻广州领事向中国两广总督抗议，要求道歉并释放亚罗号的船员。很快英军便轰炸中国沿海堡垒。

随后不久，一名法国传教士奥古斯特·沙普德莱納（中文称之为马赖神甫）在中国被处决。这使法国站在英国一边。英国在香港集结了一支庞大的军事力量后，开始与中国人开战，击沉了船队，并再次对中国清朝强加条约。在盟军和平代表团被俘虏并遭受酷刑之后，英法联军还洗劫并焚毁了老颐和园。

中国最初拒绝批准《北京公约》，这给遭受侮辱和击败的中国统治者进一步施加了压力。欧洲列强要求在封闭的北平（今北京）建立外交使团。此外，该

条约开放天津作为贸易港口，将九龙割让给了英国，允许宗教自由，使鸦片合法化，并需向英法支付巨额赔偿。

即使他们的人数比外国军队多了十倍，中国军队还是被击败了。年轻的咸丰皇帝死了，宫殿被掠夺并焚毁，昔日强大的清朝遭到羞辱和失败。只有一个前进方向：协调一致的改革、转型和现代化计划。终于在1860年开始了自强运动。从那时起，尽管常常是痛苦的而且方式也是有限的，但确实进行了一些改革。

中国正处于十字路口。亲传统主义者拒绝西方的影响和技术。反传统主义者拒绝旧的文化和方式。一个中间群体出现，希望采用西方技术，并希望通过适当的改革保留中国文明的实质。

中国由此会向何处去？

第四章　于此同时在澳大利亚

在中国历史发生重大变化的同时，随着贸易公司和欧洲商人的致富，麦世英也在不断改善自己的命运。

他将自己的名字英语化以后，现在称自己为John Shying，然后娶了一位英国女士莎拉·汤普森为妻。由于他辛勤工作和有创业精神，他得以在帕拉马塔购置土地。1829年，还获得了经营一家叫狮子的酒馆的许可证。妻子去世后，他又娶了布里奇特·吉洛里，婚礼也是在帕拉马塔的圣约翰英国国教教堂举行，该教堂是澳大利亚最古老的教堂之一。

当时，有土地的富裕家庭可以使用大量的罪犯工人。他们在服刑期间实质上是奴隶。在许多情况下，他们不是理想的工人：他们懒惰，不可靠并且常常逃跑。罪犯运输计划即将结束已有预兆，这些家庭正在寻找新工人和新的交易市场。

殖民地与中国之间的贸易早在1798年就开始了。这时，在巴伦角岛建立了熬鱼油工厂，为中国生产了近3000升海豹油，到1808至1809年，檀香木也出口到广州港口。这项不起眼且鲜为人知的贸易创业是未来中国和澳大利亚重要贸易前景的先驱。

中国被视为理想的市场，英国仍在继续进口鸦片作为贸易商品来替代白银。 这不仅为在中国的贸易租界里的英国商人带来了贸易利益，而且对大英帝国各地富裕、富有冒险精神和足智多谋的企业家来说，这是潜在的利润丰厚的收入来源。约翰·麦克阿瑟就是这样一个企业家，他在这一领域的商业兴趣早在几年前就已开始。

继1808年在悉尼发生的朗姆酒叛乱和威廉·布莱上校的受辱下台之后，麦克阿瑟和他的朋友沃尔特·戴维森启程前往伦敦，无疑是因为参与布莱起义将面对惩罚。在随后的几年中，麦克阿瑟和戴维森先是在东印度公司的帮助下，然后在著名的巴林斯贸易公司的帮助下，开始了雄心勃勃的鸦片进口业务。据我们所知，麦克阿瑟本人并未去中国。那时他在商务中保持低调，但可能正是通过这个联系，他第一次接触到了中国工人，并能够向他们提供工作还资助他们坐船来悉尼。

像麦世英这样勤奋的中国工人给麦克阿瑟及其殖民地所认识的人留下的成功印象无疑将他们的思维推向了未来，推向了一个英国罪犯遣送之后的时代。到19世纪30年代初，人们呼吁停止将罪犯遣送到澳大利亚，这使像麦克阿瑟这样的人感到紧张，因为他们长期以来一直受益于这些罪犯的劳力和服务。如果停止遣送，谁来替代这种免费劳动力来源呢？当然不是英国移民，或甚至不是解放的罪犯。麦克阿瑟认为，也许中国可以成为廉价、可靠的劳动力的来源：从中国获取劳动力可以成为一种生意。

并且，也许麦世英又名约翰·施英可以协助开展这项贸易。

事实上，约翰·施英在他的第四个儿子出生后，于1831年回了中国。他是按照麦克阿瑟的指示去开拓贸易机会还是出于家庭原因回的中国？我们永远无法知道。没有人知道他在中国去了哪里或做了什么，现已无记录留下，但他在妻子去世后于1836-37年后期回到悉尼。

随着1840年罪犯遣送结束，出现了对寻找廉价劳动力另外来源的新的呼吁，特别是中国港口的不断开放和可以进入中国内地以后。对于中国南方的那些反满族华人来说，这是逃避专制逃避社会动乱以及在其

他地方找到工作和新生活的理想途径。

来澳大利亚的中国人，可能是在麦克阿瑟-戴维森贸易安排的支持下，他们的数目细节尚不清楚。约翰·麦克阿瑟逝世几年后，在19世纪40年代似乎相当大数量的中国人来到澳大利亚。1848年10月，尼姆罗德号船在亨利·摩尔船长的带领下停泊在悉尼的米勒斯角，船上有121名来自厦门的中国人，其中一半在悉尼下船，其余的继续 乘船到维多利亚州的吉朗。在1848年至1851年间，仅悉尼的杰克逊港就有近1000名中国男子到达，第二年，这一数字上升到1600名。

社区观点立刻出现了分歧。一些人认为中国人是品德高尚值得尊敬的人，是可能替代遣送罪犯的劳动力，而另一些人则认为中国人是异国野蛮人，会引起混乱和社会问题。许多殖民者担心，如果没有妇女为男人提供稳定影响因素和陪伴，那么中国人必将对妇女实施暴力行为，造成一个不安全的社会。确实，种族主义和对’黄祸’的恐惧起源于殖民地的最早期。

麦世英于1818年抵达悉尼的时候，悉尼是一个挣扎在世界边缘的定居地，几乎没有时间来进行种族主义和歧视。老悉尼城区的街道上已经到处都是来自世界各地的面孔。因为悉尼是一个港口城市，所以这种多样性显而易见，无处不在。这种接纳将很快因为像麦世英这样具有中国血统的好公民而得到进一步巩固。华人社区工作勤奋、诚实、干净，且无犯罪。从多方面来看他们都是理想的公民。

但是，在中国以及随后不久在整个太平洋地区发生的事件将极大地影响来澳大利亚的中国移民。在中国内部，社会动荡和流血正在造成越来越多的移民潮。人们渴望摆脱农村的流离失所、贫困、社会动荡和未来的不确定性。这种华人的大流散开始体现在1849年在加利福尼亚的金矿地区，1851年后的澳大利亚以及加拿大和美国的铁路建设行业中。中国人在移

动，寻找新的机会，新的财富和更安全的生活。

加州的淘金热始于1848年1月。在萨克拉曼多东部科洛莫的萨特磨坊发现了黄金，1849年，第一批的50名中国矿工来到了这里。很快，有300,000人从美国和其他地区涌到这里，其中包括20,000中国人，这些人全部从旧金山向内地进发。中国国民的到来一直持续到1887年，当时美国有150,000多人，其中116,000人在加利福尼亚。外国船东宣扬激动人心的发现、神话般的新财富以及世界上发现金矿和发财的地方的消息，极大地激发了人们的热情。这确保了他们的船只迅速装满了乐观的矿工、他们的工具和财产以及贸易商品。

到达美国后，中国人提供了流向金矿的人空缺出来的服务和工作。在早期，中国人受到欢迎。他们提供劳动力、服务和开零售店； 他们当家庭佣人、洗衣工、厨师、木匠和商店售货员。他们被认为是勤劳、诚实、干净和不惹眼的人。虽然在社交和习俗上很不同，但他们被公认为是未来的好公民和平等的社会成员。中国人欢迎这个新世界、工作机会、食物以及他们逃避了饥饿、战争和社会动荡这一事实。这儿也是可以给在中国的家庭汇钱的收入来源。

然而，当他们前往金矿时，怒恨和蔑视很快就清楚地显露了出来。美国矿工将中国人视为是来抢’他们的’黄金，在他们认为应该是他们才有权的地方开采潜在的含金矿藏。这转化为对和平、勤劳的中国矿工的骚扰和暴力，甚至死亡。中国矿工的营地被毁，他们的财产被盗。

到了1850年，即发现黄金仅两年后，加利福尼亚州立法对所有非美国矿工征收20美元的税，这在当时是一笔很大的数目。然后，1853-54年采矿业的衰落和崩溃以及随后许多企业的倒闭，都被怪罪于中国人。一些华人搬到新的铁路工地，成为铁路建设的重

要劳动力，遍及美国和加拿大。 然而，一旦开始，种族歧视、种族隔离和暴力便继续下去。直到20世纪20 年代，立法才决定了这些勤劳的人们的命运、他们继续采矿的能力以及他们进入美国的机会。

在澳大利亚，中国移民在19世纪30年代末和40年代继续少量入境。从英国遣送来的罪犯的流量正在枯竭，对劳动力的需求变得迫切。中国人填补了这一缺口，很快成为仅次于英国和德国人的第三大种族群体。

首先是在新南威尔士州然后在维多利亚州发现了黄金，这触发了中国人到澳大利亚的大量增加。这个消息很快随着金山和即刻发财的故事传遍了中国。到澳大利亚后，矿工们成群结队跋涉到金矿区，其中一些人随身携带了一些可卖的物品，例如镐、铁锹、基本衣物、帐篷和采矿必需品。他们不是仅专注于黄金，而是开发生意：他们开餐馆，开零售商店和洗衣服务，为采矿社区提供了必要的服务。

但是，从一开始，中国人就感到不受欢迎，生命受到威胁。与加利福尼亚州的金矿区一样，中国人被视为’窃取’了白人的黄金，尽管他们的许多工作是重新加工尾矿和先前采矿中遗留下来的废渣堆。中国矿工成组一起工作，住在不同的营地，从一开始，他们就不仅受到矿工，而且受到政府和官方行政部门的排斥和欺凌。

1853年，在维多利亚中国人最大的营地，人数从2,000人激增至20,000人。骚乱和不满情绪蔓延。维多利亚州政府在1855年试图通过第一个反华立法来限制移民。这包括在抵达时收取10英镑的人头税。为避免这种情况，中国人改为在其他澳大利亚港口，例如南澳大利亚的罗布（Robe）港入境，然后步行到维多利亚的金矿区。看到这项立法失败了，维多利亚州政府接下来对中国矿工实行了特别的许可证，进一步加

剧了紧张和歧视。

根据维多利亚州的模式，南澳大利亚州和新南威尔士州也制定了类似的法律。 中国矿工被拒绝入籍。 在1860年至1861年之间，新南威尔士州扬市附近爆发了一系列严重骚乱-产羔牧场暴乱，据估计虽然没有人丧生但有1,000名中国人受伤。到了1867年，淘金热几乎结束，反华法律被废除。 大多数中国寻金者回到中国，其余的中国人以勤劳、诚实和善良的公民身份融入澳大利亚社会。

然而，中国人仍然被吸引来澳大利亚。他们首先前往达尔文，是在1869年对城镇所在地进行调查后，当时该地区的华人人口接近200，而欧洲人只有600。两年后，他们前往了位于松树溪的新发现的金矿区。新的机遇带来了新的移民，这些移民改变了北澳大利亚的面貌和种族构成。

第五章 新世界里的中国

于此同时，中国动荡不安的情况继续。从1861年开始，通过狡猾的手段和操纵，慈禧太后击败了她的敌人和密谋者，巩固了自己的权力。她让自己五岁的儿子登基作皇帝，在咸丰皇帝兄弟的支持下，处决了挑战她权力和控制的八大顾命大臣中的三位（其余革职）。她掌握权力以后的第一件事是检查官员的工作，这是一种程序，每隔三年来自全国各地的官员来汇报前一阶段的工作进展情况。通过确保全国省级以上的官员都直接向她个人报告，从而增加权力和控制。为了加强她的控制，她处死了三位怀疑有罪的官员，在这过程中实现了对权力的铁腕控制。

然而，中国在第二次鸦片战争中被打败以后，皇太后慈禧认识到是改变的时候了。欧洲列强的军事技术优势表明以一个农村和农业为基础的经济无法与一个以工业和技术为基础的经济竞争，必须变革。这时，学者和前瞻性思维的官员开始了一系列的改革，包括建设工厂、机器厂、造船厂、棉纺厂、加强出口业务的蒸汽轮船公司、语言学校、教育机构、以及海军学院和军事学院。甚至派年轻人出国学习经验和培训，希望以此通过西方方式来振新中国。但是儒家传统仍根深蒂固，一般认为这些传统是中国在军事和经济上面对西方和创造新中国时的问题根源。

1818年中国再次陷入战争。这次是与法国。法国看中了印度支那，即现代的越南，而中国支持越南。在1885年6月签署的和平条约中，法国成功地得到了交趾支那、柯钦察、安南和东京的领土，但法国多次交战失败给中国带来了新的希望和新的军事信心。法国人放弃了福摩萨（今天的台湾），但他们实现了大部分的其他领土目标。对中国而言，幸运的是，给法

国带来的政治损失削弱了其未来的殖民统治计划。

在中国这一冲突进一步削弱了清朝的力量，促使强大的民族主义运动重新出现。因为努力实现现代化和集中军事指挥，在试图使军事指挥现代化和集中化的过程中，持续不断的军事失败，特别是海军失败是令人感到羞辱的事。他们进一步降低了皇太后和大清王朝的权力和威望。

除了军事失败以外，慈禧还得处理各种互相冲突的利害关系和要求变革的压力。例如，清廷相信铁路是很聪明但是无用之物，因此慈禧禁止建造。这种过时的思维导致了犹豫不决、举措不定、缺乏信息和缺乏远见，扼杀了当时急需的果断行动。而她继续挥霍无度，不管不顾深刻变革的必要，包括采用西方做事和思维的方式的必要。

在欧洲和美国政府和商人集中注意打开中国的门户的时候，在邻近的日本也在发生相似的情况。佩里准将于1853年和1854年远征之前日本从来未遭到过严重挑战。与中国不同，日本很快看到与西方通商的潜在益处。1854年3月日本签订了一个条约，对美国商人开放了下田和函馆的港口，允许建立美国外交使团，并为遭海难的美国水手提供照管。

中国和日本都有悠久的孤立主义历史，并严格限制了贸易和西方的渗透。 中国最初欢迎贸易，但仅限于在广州挑选的中国商人，而日本只允许在出岛港口与荷兰人进行贸易。然而，当佩里准将在1854年强迫日本向美国敞开大门时，中国已经过贸易租界和贸易港口的压力导致战争的经历。日本能够看到欧洲列强的运作方式、他们的军事技术能力以及这些机会可以带来什么。

如我们所见，中国对西方国家和西方文化的接受和理解很缓慢。人们向内看，只阅读过时且不相关的正统文本。他们与外国人的接触仅限于贸易场所，而日本人则积极研究西方的方法，甚至翻译了西方的书籍，从而鼓励了进一步的研究和讨论。

日本接受了西方商人和技术，迅速成为一个工业化国家，吸引了外国技术人员来教授和管理新的工业基础设施。这些变化带来了新的行政管理系统、金融机制和造币、税收以及政治和经济管理，所有这些都为国家立即带来了直接利益。日本还制定了宪法，赋予帝国议会立法权。作为明治寡头政治运动的一部分，改革者和未来主义思想家们努力在一个以英国和普鲁士政府为基础的松散模型中融合了君主立宪制和君主专制。

第六章 在遥远的澳大利亚

这些政治经济和社会变化在澳大利亚没有人注意到也不为人知。然而，令人吃惊的是澳大利亚和中国之间开始了一股贸易的涓涓细流：大型羊毛经纪戈尔兹伯勒公司于1875年开始向上海出口羊毛。随后很快就有船运生铅，当时是用于茶箱的衬里。冷藏带来了食品出口的新机会，特别是冷冻肉和苹果等新鲜农产品，这打开了包括日本在内的新市场。种族和歧视问题被遗忘了：贸易和商业推动着新的关系。

据信年纪已老的约翰·施英1880年6月去世。到这个时候，他应该已经比较富裕了，并且肯定与麦克阿瑟和布拉克斯兰家族有很好的联系。考虑到他在中国和澳大利亚的关系网络，他似乎很可能以某种方式参与了早期的进出口贸易。

与美国一样，澳大利亚在接纳和吸收来年轻的国家找到新家的华人方面也非常缓慢，对华人仍然有恐惧感余味。华人的工作方式、生活方式、东方的态度以及澳大利亚的种族歧视主导着对华人的态度并深深影响着移民政策。这种态度出现在1863年后举行的一系列澳亚殖民地会议上，当时所有国家都起草并同意了中国移民政策的原则。这些会议是在昆士兰州和西澳大利亚州新发现金矿的背景下举行的，再次对华人移民设置了限制：法律禁止华人矿工入籍。

这种反华情感在继续着。1887年5月在悉尼市政厅举行的大型示威游行要求限制中国移民，可接受的入籍种类很少。1888年，《中国人限制与管理法》成为法律，随后其他州也颁布了类似的立法。对大量来自北方的中国人的恐惧在南澳大利亚如此强烈，以至于所有跨越达尔文以南1000英里处的一条假想的界线的中国人加收10英镑的税。只有塔斯马尼亚州对中国人有同情心，既允许中国人家庭进入，也允许入籍程

序，但这最终被联邦《1903年入籍法》所阻止。

然而，在华人创业、贡献和文化产品方面仍然存在着大量但鲜为人知的遗产。澳大利亚常见的俗语’fair dinkum’中’dinkum’来自中文单词’din’和’ kum’，意为真实或真正的金子。澳大利亚人现在仍然使用此短语来形容任何真实、真正、非伪造的或典型澳大利亚的任何事物。它的起源来自中文，这也许会让许多澳大利亚人感到惊讶。

同样令人惊讶的是，此时有一位澳大利亚记者成为中国关系和报道动荡不安的中华民族事件的重要人物。乔治·莫里森曾在墨尔本大学和爱丁堡大学学习，是一名医学毕业生。1894年他担任《伦敦时报》的记者，开始了他既是记者又是中国事务顾问的杰出职业生涯。他影响了中国历史的进程二十年。

在此期间，莫里森报道了中国的所有重大事件：由光绪皇帝领导的百日维新，义和团运动，1904-1905年的日俄战争和俄国舰队的失败以及推翻了清朝的1911年革命。后来他成为袁世凯总统的顾问。莫里森参加了1919年的凡尔赛和平会议。他对将山东省移交给日本而不是还给中国而如此出卖中国的行为感到极为震惊。

莫里森还是早期提倡与中国增加贸易关系的人。以他命名的莫里森讲座由悉尼和墨尔本的澳大利亚华人于1932年建立，至今仍每年在堪培拉举行，旨在增进对中国文化、文学和艺术的了解，相信对文化的了解会促进贸易的增长。

后来效仿莫里森的是一位同样了不起的澳大利亚人威廉·唐纳德（William Donald）。他也是《伦敦时报》和其他报纸的记者。他1911-12年为孙中山短暂的政府担任顾问。唐纳德也是蒋介石及其妻子宋美龄的朋友，也是国民党领导人张学良的顾问。

1937年日本入侵中国后，唐纳德与蒋介石夫人一起开展了有效的公共关系活动，帮助改变美国的孤立主义政策并获得美国对中国抗日的支持。在世界各地的《生活》杂志、《波士顿先驱报》和《纽约时报》杂志以及悉尼的《每日电讯报》上都刊登了蒋介石夫人的频繁报道。

随着新世纪的到来，澳大利亚成为了自己的国家。少数中国人留在了这儿，但残留的恐惧和不信任感主导着澳大利亚对移民的态度。这种恐惧最终体现在新国家议会的第一年便通过了臭名昭著的《1901年移民限制法》，通常称为’白澳政策’。

在其简短的殖民历史中，澳大利亚经历了巨大的变化、内部分歧、发现以及经济和政治变革。对内地进行了探索和非神秘化，土著居民被控制，矿藏财富得到发现和开发。繁荣、萧条和干旱已经确立了一种生死周期，澳大利亚也小心翼翼地迈入了新世纪。

第七章　日本问题

与日本人不同的是，中国的清朝根本就不明白仅对传统方式做些微小改变是不够的，也不明白由于西方工业革命造成了传统西方社会深刻的结构变化，西方也面临过重大的社会和经济混乱。中国人将西方人视为野蛮人，而中国才是文化和文明的中心，这与日本人的态度再次大相径庭。

长期以来，对朝鲜的控制一直是中日之间紧张的根源。从19世纪70年代开始，日本曾试图迫使朝鲜开放贸易，但朝鲜一直处于清朝的保护和影响之下。日本的压力使裂痕很快进一步扩大，1882年出现了一场危机，两国之间签署了一项关于共享控制权和贸易准入的条约，才化解了这一危机。同时，日本正在根据欧洲的战术和指挥结构建立一支庞大的、现代的、装备由欧洲供给的海军和陆军。而中国却在做恰恰相反的事：减少军费开支，信任其传统防御和一支过时的海军和陆军。

经过十年在朝鲜控制问题上的争论不休，日本军队后来占领了汉城，并在朝鲜半岛周围进行海军封锁，最后战争终于在1894年8月爆发。在随后的八个月中，战争继续进行，在一系列失败之后，中国人与日本签署了一项条约，将朝鲜、台湾岛和其他领土的控制权移交给日本，并同意赔偿。该条约还允许日本船只在扬子江（今长江）上贸易，并开放贸易港口和制造工厂。中国再次被羞辱，而这次是被一个亚洲邻国而不是一个欧洲大国羞辱。辽东半岛的丢失也使日本在满洲有了立足之地，成为日本在1931年入侵满洲的起点。

在中国屈膝的情况下，其他欧洲大国争先恐后地通过势力范围和贸易让步夺取中国的份额。这加剧了

中国人对其被外国人接管和征服的恐惧，进而导致了对清朝进行改革的进一步要求。

面对一系列艰难的选择，慈禧太后决定支持反对洋人的义和团，也被称为义和拳。他们是一个狂热团体，相信自己拥有使子弹转向的神奇力量。这些激进组织起初是为了在中国摆脱基督教传教士并杀害中国基督教徒的基础上发展起来的，但后来，尤其是在19世纪90年代后期，随着中国’瓜’的瓜分之后，又发展成为反对洋人的势力。

不出所料，对基督教传教士的袭击引起了欧洲国家的愤怒，欧洲国家派遣部队保护教堂以及他们的利益和特权。随着反对洋人的暴力升级以及八国联军的到来，义和团运动在中国东部大部分地区爆发。1900年6月至1900年8月期间，义和团包围了北京的外国使馆，但他们无法将洋人赶出中国。中国再次面临失败，面临外国列强强加的毁灭性赔偿债务。

这时，澳大利亚意外地因为义和团运动与中国发生了联系。它在北京没有领事馆，但应英国海军部的要求，派遣了200名称作’蓝夹克’的水兵以及来自新南威尔士的轻步兵50名士兵和一些海军舰艇。他们于1900年8月启航前往香港，但由于到达为时已晚，未能参加保护和解放使馆的活动。该部队作为占领军的一部分一直呆到1901年4月，承担支援的角色，负责运送物资和人员。

中国战败最终使人们听到了改革和现代化的声音。正是义和团运动为中国政府和社会的深刻重组提供了导火线，这种重组将在未来50年内继续下去。

随着二十世纪的到来，变革，改革和新的、强大的中国开始从灰烬中崛起。

第八章 新旧冲突

在中国遭受传统与现代化的争斗之苦之时，欧洲也是如此。在欧洲，旧的方式在为新的方式让路，传统的以土地为基础的社会在让位给工业化和城市的发展。古老而稳固的贵族面对着工业化带来的新贵（暴发户），这些新贵的财富来自采矿、钢铁、银行、制造业和军备。人们大批从农村搬到城市，或是被围地运动赶出了土地，或是受到新的工作和机会的吸引。随着城市的扩大，贫困加剧。广泛流离失所的创伤带来了巨大的变化，也带来了新的社会主义运动，带来了工会主义和大规模的贫困与苦难。

但是，中国的处境远为更加严峻和糟糕。到19世纪末，中国作为一个民族被击败，被羞辱，在文化上也遭耻辱。虽然清朝还在苟延残喘，慈禧太后仍然保留着名义上的控制权，但中国已变成了一个与50年前大不相同的国家。由于战败而被迫向西方开放，它仍然存在分歧，在前进的方向上仍是困惑不清。它面临着一个难题：面临着中国传统与现代改革要求的矛盾。

尽管要求改革的呼声坚持不断无处不在，但占统治地位的清朝仍然坚决抵制变革。慈禧太后与清廷的许多人不仅担心失去权力，而且还认为中国的伟大之处在于其悠久的控制权和传统的过去。1898年，年轻的光绪皇帝经历了戊戌变法的失败，这是在改革者、知识分子和文化精英的影响下进行的短暂变革尝试。慈禧太后毫不含糊地拒绝了他的改革，不久之后，在慈禧的命令下，他被软禁，要他死于年纪轻轻，不会再进一步介入中国历史。

义和团运动期间，慈禧皇太后着装农民式样逃离北京到西安（丝绸之路的起点和兵马俑博物馆的所在地）。在欧洲军队又一次打败中国屈辱中国之后，慈

禧回到了首都北京。尽管她曾积极支持被击败的义和团，但她仍然逃脱了惩罚。

很快，慈禧终于试图开展一些有限的改革，但这些改革实在是太少也太迟了。更大和重要的问题是如上所述取消具有2000年历史的儒家科举制度。她派朝廷官员前往欧洲和日本了解外国的方式，为起草对中国社会、政府、法律制度、教育和行政管理作大规模的变革作准备。具有讽刺意味的是，许多类似的改革建议都是那些在戊戌变法失败后被她处死的人士在1898年向她提出过的。

改革方案是广泛且多样的。它改善了法律制度，减少了残酷和暴力的惩罚，允许铁路的现代化，改革了货币、国民经济和政府，并在军队内部进行了改革，建立新的国家军队。教育也得到改善，新的西式学校教授西方的课程 。

慈禧试图与居住在首都的外国人接触，特别是外交使节的夫人们。她在新建的颐和园举办早茶，甚至同意由一位美国画家为她画肖像，以参加1904年的圣路易斯世界博览会。这都是新中国的一部分，但新兴的革命和变革力量已经逼近。

1908年11月中旬，濒临死亡之时，报仇心重的慈溪要做的最后一项任务是：灭掉光绪皇帝。她担心光绪皇帝会扭转自己的改革之路，并像他在1898年所尝试的那样，在中国社会和政府内部进行更为激进的变革。给他食用了大量的砒霜后，光绪帝于11月14日去世。在这同一天里，慈禧扶持了两岁的溥仪作为新皇帝。第二天，即11月15日，她也去世了。

慈禧太后去世后，清朝终于瓦解。在此期间，著名的思想家、改革家和政治鼓动者开始拥护新政

选择，他们已决定传统的满族帝国制度已经过时，西方式的民主制度是一种更合适的政府制度。由此产生了对新中国的理想，在这一理想的新中国，传统思想与新的方式综合或被完全抛弃。这成为永不休止的争论：如何使中国现代化并保留传统文化价值和传统信仰。

第九章 旧中国的新方向

当时的一位主要思想家和革命家是孙中山，也称孙逸仙。他出生于广州附近一个贫穷的农村家庭，在香港和夏威夷的传教会学校受的教育。后来他学习医学并成为了医生，但是不久之后，由于受到秘密社团成员身份和在国外的影响，他开始转向政治。1894年，孙中山成立了复兴会，由学生和中国秘密社团的成员构成。次年，作为复兴会的领导，他协助组织了失败的广州反帝大起义。此后，他流亡国外16年，直到1911年才返回中国。到那时，持不同政见者已经草拟了实行民主进程的时间表，其中包括君主立宪制和议会制。

慈禧死后，由此产生了权力真空，推翻清朝和建立新共和国的时机已经成熟。1908年至1911年之间，全国各地成立了各种革命团体，其目标范围从有限的变革到彻底推翻统治精英集团和建立共和国。在这些年中，针对溥仪统治下的清廷残余不断发生起义、造反和暴动。

最早的反清组织起源于中国境外，通常是如孙中山先生那样的爱国人士、知识分子和政治异见人士，他们观察国外的方式，并根据自己的经历塑造了对新中国的愿景。他们回国以后，通常对实现民主变革有着截然不同的看法和方式。有些人通过改变传统价值观而建树；还有其他人则通过无政府状态、恐怖主义、暴力和暗杀来寻求激进的手段。从这些范围广泛的群体中，涌现出了未来的政治和社会领袖。

最终摊牌的起因是湖北省武昌的一场铁路纠纷。省政府无力支付建设费用，因此寻求外国贷款，引起了广大民众的不满，开始骚乱。当地反抗力量变得强大后，清朝派兵来平息暴动，而这是极不受欢迎的举动，导致了大规模集会、广泛罢工和更坚定的抵抗。

在保路同志会的领导人被捕，军队并向示威者开枪后，广大人民参加了反抗，攻击政府和地方当局，危机进一步升级。

孙中山从新闻报道中听到有关武昌起义成功的消息后于1911年12月下旬从美国回到中国。他在南京的一次会议上当选为临时总统,1912年1月1日被命名为中华民国新临时政府的首日。他在就职宣誓中保证’倾覆满洲专制政府，巩固中华民国，图谋民生幸福’。

此时的清朝仍然是不可忽视的力量，因为没有军事力量打败旧政权，孙中山被迫与北洋军司令袁世凯将军进行谈判。如果袁能够说服清朝皇帝退位，或者逼他下台，孙就将总统位置移交给袁。袁向年轻的溥仪皇帝施加压力，溥仪皇帝退位以换取他和他的母亲隆裕太后的安全保障。袁在1912年2月12日完成这个任务。

孙中山履行与袁世凯达成的协议，袁世凯于1912年2月成为临时总统，并于同年3月10日宣誓就职。因此，孙中山任总统期间的相对平静是短暂短命的。孙不久就发现袁世凯无视共和国的理想，草拟的临时宪法几乎被遗忘。相反，他用暴政和军事力量统治，甚至解散了执政的组织国民党，并以死威胁新参议员。到1915年，袁世凯宣布自己为皇帝，但面对普遍的抵抗和军事支持的丧失，他只得下台。第二年他就去世。

当中国努力战胜旧政权并在许多提议、模型和理论中寻找合适的、可行的替代方案时，在中国境外紧张的局势正在加剧。殖民地和贸易租界的竞赛虽然实际上已经结束了，但却在世界范围内留下了与中国一样深刻的殖民地破坏和流离失所的痕迹。所有这些都是在欧洲发生类似的社会动乱和动荡的背景下发生的。

第十章 远离中国的新的紧张局势

国际紧张局势挑战着各地的旧秩序。正如欧洲的贸易港口竞争已深深地影响了旧中华帝国一样，这些同样的欧洲国家正在改变世界各地，他们强迫非工业化往往是部落的国家服从，控制它们的经济、财富、资源及其人民。

为了满足这一贸易和帝国的要求，需要海运并需要海军保护海运。于是为了捍卫它们的贸易路线以及食品和原材料的生命线又开始了一场庞大的海军竞赛，特别是在英国和德国之间。随之而来的就是需要港口，因此德国人在山东省建立了租借条约下的青岛港。

这对英国海军是个直接挑战，特别是来自德国的挑战，从而造成了紧张局势。现在各国结盟，签署条约，并希望重新武装自己。德国担心被包围，与奥地利和意大利结成了同盟。法国人与俄罗斯和英国结成同盟。巴尔干半岛这个火绒箱，尤其是朽败的哈普斯堡帝国，也在增加紧张气氛：奥地利转向德国寻求支持，属于哈普斯堡帝国一部分的塞尔维亚帝国的斯拉夫人民向俄罗斯求助。日益严重的世界危机很快就不在政治家和君主掌控之下，进入到威胁与反威胁的循环之中。

世界正走向不可避免的战争碰撞过程中。中国也将不会幸免。

随着西方大国在1913年和1914年初接近战争，中国意识到交战国可能将其四分五裂，一方面有英国、法国、俄罗斯和美国的外交代表团、贸易港口和特许权，另一方面也与德国有同样的关系。这些海外大国在对待中国方面也有自己的同盟，例如英国和日本之间的联盟，而后者又牵涉到法国和俄罗斯。尽管德国

仍避免建立这种联盟，但胶澳（胶州）湾作为贸易中心和战略港口对于目前已在亚太地区巡逻的德国海军来说是非常重要的。如果德国输掉了战争，中国人可能可以重新收回这些租借地。美国也参与其中，但在1914年7月至8月宣战之前，美国仍然坚持超然远离不作表态，不懈地奉行开放的贸易政策，孤立主义的外交政策。

社会内部的混乱，对传统方式的强迫改变，新的工业化以及随之而来的贫困，使欧洲开始分裂，各国因分裂而恐惧，因此被迫结成同盟。衰败的奥地利哈普斯堡帝国向德国寻求支持，以反对其在现称为南斯拉夫的顽劣的斯拉夫国家。法国、俄罗斯和英国结成了自己的联盟和条约以相互支持。

到1914年，世界已经失去控制，肯定是已经失去了欧洲国王和摄政王的控制。奥地利王位继承人弗朗兹·费迪南大公被暗杀后，点燃了第一次世界大战的导火线。中国只能无能为力地退缩。但是欧洲国家也是如此：一切已为时过晚。1914年8月4日，德国在入侵法国的路上跨过比利时边境后，英国向德国宣战。

这种战争般的回旋调动、战略操纵和威胁的广阔背景，是在过去的一百多年里在中国经历混乱而屈辱的历史背景下发生的。要了解中国，就要了解最近的动荡历史：新与旧之间的紧张局势，外国人的入侵，战争和饥荒造成了巨大的生命损失和对未来的巨大不确定性。

这段历史和动荡与外国干预直接相关。现在，进一步的动荡以及可能在中国领土上进行的欧洲战争的威胁对新的中国领导层来说是十分令人焦虑的事。

第十一章 艰难的选择

战争的乌云在逼近，欧洲人在中国和邻近海域的调遣，中国意识到必须迅速宣布中立。1914年8月6日，英国宣战的两天之后，中国政府宣布中立，并警告外国不得在中国任何地方进行军事行动。这份声明说，这是一场欧洲战争，是帝国主义大国之间的冲突，这些帝国主义大国曾经压制和摧毁了传统中国，并曾给中国带来了极大的悲痛和屈辱。

日本人无意尊重中国人的中立要求。8月15日，即宣战不到两周后，日本要求德国人在9月15日之前撤出德国胶州租借地，并在8月23日对德国宣战。因此，日本成为反对德国的盟国之一。

此后不久，在英国的帮助下，日本又封锁了胶州湾。几周后，日军在龙口附近登陆，从那儿进驻了德国旧殖民区。到11月，德国人投降并被日本俘虏，许多人被俘关押至1919年。尽管中国人抗议反对这场战争，但这是整个第一次世界大战期间唯一在中国土地上进行的陆战或战争行为。

尽管中国幸运没有积极参与这场战争，但在远东的海战突然使中国卷入其中。这可以追溯到19世纪90年代中期，当时德国人组建了东亚舰队。该舰队主要在太平洋运作，是一个独立的舰队，是德国唯一不以本国港口为母港运作的舰队。1897年，德国人攻克占领了在胶州湾的中国防御工事。次年，他们根据所谓的胶州湾租借地迫使清朝将面积552平方公里的土地割让给德国。这是对胶州湾周围地区长达99年的租约，其中包括青岛这个小渔村，当时那里街道是狭窄的土路，房屋破旧易倒。

德国人立即开始大兴土木，建造了政府大楼和欧式房屋，提供了电力和淡水。在港口区，德国人建造

了码头和船坞，仓库和武器库，为后来成为远东舰队的基地提供设施。由此，舰队的补给、补煤和修理基地有了保障，德国人就能够在整个太平洋地区进行行动。

英国宣战的第二天，澳大利亚跟着宣战。战争动员立即开始，全国各地的招募台都挤满了激情的志愿者。澳大利亚很快答应向欧洲战场提供2万名士兵，并派遣一支远征部队前往北部的德属新几内亚的德国殖民地，那里长途电台将德国的本国舰队与他们在东方的基地连接起来，特别是与中国的青岛相连。

因此，在1914年的上半年，德国人在中国和日本海域进行了一系列巡游。宣战以后，他们立即转向攻击性行动。1914年7月31日，埃姆登号小巡洋舰出海，三天后，也就是与俄罗斯宣战后的第二天，俘获了俄罗斯的蒸汽船梁赞号，并将其拖回青岛。

这次事件之后，埃姆登号再次从青岛出发。在随后的三个月中，它进行了一次惊人的破坏之旅，击沉并俘获了两艘协约国军舰和16艘轮船。在一次大胆的突袭中，埃姆登号驶入马德拉斯港，摧毁了燃油箱和港口设施。从那里出来，埃姆登沿途沉没了许多船只，还对英属马来亚的槟城进行了突击袭击，摧毁了正在维修中的俄罗斯巡洋舰詹姆查克号，并在离开港口时沉没了另一艘法国驱逐舰木斯克号。

到这时，埃姆登号已成为一艘被追捕的舰船，她离青岛母港也很远。与此同时青岛母港已被日本人占领。埃姆登的船长卡尔·冯·穆勒决定攻占科科斯群岛的英国广播电台，与此同时还诱走了英国海军舰艇，据说这些海军舰船正在印度洋北部寻找埃姆登。

该舰船靠近该岛的行动被无线站工作人员观察到，他们发出信号：’身份不明的船只正在入港’。澳大利亚轻型巡洋舰悉尼号接到了信号，那时她正护

送第一批澳大利亚部队前往埃及。悉尼号约在50海里（80公里）以外。它迅速转北，驶往埃姆登所在的地方。经过一场战火悬殊的战斗之后，埃姆登号被驱赶到科科斯群岛，在那里她被大炮摧毁，剩余船员被俘。从此结束了从青岛港出海的所有海军和军事行动，并使中国摆脱了在其海岸进一步作战的威胁。

随着欧洲战争的隆隆声，中国对世界及她在其中所处位置的看法产生了变化。新的民族主义和新的国际主义开始超越传统观念。这是由内部出现的反传统观点以及前所未有的需要接触世界和国际事务的需求所培育发展起来的。中国意识到的这场国际战争将产生深远而持久的影响：它为中国提供了新的机会，使中国可以平等的成员国身份加入世界秩序。

因此，对于中国人来说，下一个问题是：如何参与这场战争，以及这种参与的最终结果是什么？普遍的看法是，战争将在圣诞节前结束，德国要么将在法国和俄罗斯迅速取得胜利，而且在此过程中，多年来侵犯中国的主要罪犯英国也将被击败。

另外，同盟国，法国、英国和俄罗斯也可能会取得胜利。这将使中国从胶州湾租借地特许中解脱。但是中国意识到，在短期内，它必须不采取任何行动，远离她没有参与也没有影响的战争。无论谁赢了，中国都将摆脱其对失败国所做的让步承诺，并赢得一个新起点，可以沿着西方的、非传统路线建设战后的新中国。

正是怀着这一长远目标，袁世凯将军开始与英国首相约翰·乔登接触。他愿提供50,000名士兵参加联合行动，夺回青岛，并拖延日军实现在其领土上的野心。乔登拒绝了任何此类的倡议，但中国人再次向英国寻求帮助，尤其是在日本于1915年1月向中国提出’二十一条要求’之后。这些苛刻的日本条款迫使中国进一步成为她的附庸国及原材料和产品的来源

地。这自然将中国的注意力集中在近期的战争和未来的和平会议上。对于中国而言，面临的挑战是如何在和平会议桌上赢得一席之地以及实现这一目标的最佳途径。

第十二章　支持一方

中国现在必须决定支持哪一方。同盟军似乎是可能的胜利者，但现在是中国主要敌人的日本却站在同盟军的一边。解决这一可怕矛盾的答案在于中国迫切需要国际地位和认可。必须找到一种一方面参与战争，但另一方面保持其宣布的中立的方式。怎么才能做到呢？

这项新政策和创新思想的声音是一位杰出而有影响力的政治家梁士诒。梁通过在官场服务，在铁路方面具有特别的经验。他提供了深刻、宝贵的理解和有权的朋友。他是袁世凯的知己，他对外交政策的前瞻性看法以及对欧洲战争将为未来中国提供巨大机遇的信念能够影响将军。除了建议结束义和团运动的赔款和恢复山东省的建议外，他还提出中国参与战争的各种可选方式。

梁士诒意识到中国需要以军事以外的其他形式加入战争，因此提出了许多方法。他的目标是提高中国的国际声誉，摆脱其可耻的过去并确立其未来地位。意识到中国无法派遣军队，他迅速提出了一项计划，该计划不是基于军事援助而是基于劳力。首先，通过派遣体力劳动者，中国可以在不违背中立原则的情况下为盟国提供支持。其次，通过表面上称为’私营’公司的劳务承包，中国可以支持盟军的战争努力，但仍能反驳指责其违反宣称中立的指控。

英法两国都拒绝了中国的援助，甚至无视梁的劳力计划和主动要提供帮助的意愿。但西线的流血消耗和同盟国盟军的人员严重短缺改变了他们的看法。到1914年底，在法国人勉强挽救了巴黎，伤亡人数达到30万人之后，随着对立的前线开始长期停滞的战争，迫切需要来自另一个地方的帮助。梁士诒的提议现在看来很有可取之处，在同盟国中，尤其是法国人心中

形成了中国劳工分队的基本构想。

对中国人而言，这是对盟军战争努力作光荣、谨慎和有计划的贡献，值得将来考虑和认可。对于法国人和英国人以及后来的俄罗斯人来说，这是在战争中出乎意料的援助来源，在这场战争中后勤、供应和协调至关重要。

一切皆准备就绪。

第十三章　澳大利亚去参战

回到澳大利亚，早期的征兵工作是非常有选择性的。他们拒绝了有扁平足和牙齿不好的人。他们拒绝了具有中国传统的澳大利亚人。1909年的《国防法》规定，'非相当程度上是欧洲血统或欧洲后裔的人'将免于参加前线任务。除此以外，还有一个条件，'只应招募在相当程度上是欧洲血统的英国臣民'。也有身体要求，但是随着增援需要的增加，这些要求很快降低。身材矮小的中国男人现在可以在士兵队伍中找到一席之地。各种个人档案都有列出身高不足5英尺2英寸（152厘米）的人。

尽管多年来遭受虐待和种族歧视，并有立法在阻止他们参军入伍，但华人社区支持国家的战争努力。华人媒体鼓励华裔澳大利亚人入伍参战，并刊登广告鼓励华人社区为战争贷款捐款。他们还为战争慰问基金捐款，为红十字会筹款，并为回国伤员提供福利。

华裔男子也加入了入伍队伍。许多人是第二代和第三代土生土长的澳大利亚人，他们几乎没有什么特征可以表明有中国血统，名字也非中国人名字。在征募的241名澳大利亚华人中，62人的名字听起来是盎格鲁传统的；179人名字的一部分（通常是姓）是中文。

有时他们有中国血统这点可能很明显，很多时征兵中心的官员很可能是知道他们是有中国血统的。但澳大利亚帝国部队需要优秀的人，医生和征兵人员都对他们的血统来自何处是视而不见的。在这些应征者的军队个人档案中，尤其是在'特殊标记'标题下，没有提及任何中国特色或身体特征。

早期的典型新兵是来自维多利亚州的华裔澳大利亚人乔治·格里菲斯（George Griffiths），他于1914年8月18日入伍，在宣战仅两周以后。他是一位

矿工，年龄30岁，单身，身高5英尺7英寸，来自巴拉瑞特北边的塔尔伯特。他所在的第8营在宣战后的两周内在维多利亚乡村成立。由于他的士兵序列号低，格里菲斯应是很早就应征的兵。

格里菲斯于1914年11月离开墨尔本，在去加里波利之前驻扎在埃及。他参加了在克里西亚的攻击战，他所在的营在1915年5月8日一天中有217人伤亡，随后不久他也受伤并被救离。1916年，他去法国，在帕斯尚尔战役附近遭毒气，但后来康复并在1919年初返回澳大利亚。

其他人则没有那么幸运。维克托·列普（Victor Lepp）是1915年入伍的三个华裔澳大利亚人兄弟之一。他们来自巴拉瑞特，是中国矿工的后裔。三兄弟都去了埃及，维克多参加了加里波利战役，然后去了西线。1916年8月下旬在波济耶尔，他所在的营’在白垩坑和前线之间执行任务’时，他不幸战死。他的两个兄弟于1919年返回澳大利亚。

也许最著名的澳纽军团华裔战士是威廉·’比利’·辛，他是一名管马人，于1914年10月在博恩入伍。比利的父亲是华人约翰·辛，是上海人，当时40岁，比利的母亲叫玛丽·安·皮尤，是英国人，来自英国的斯塔福德，当时30岁。他在农村长大，十二岁就离开了就缀学，努力工作养家。他坚韧，足智多谋，善于驾驭马，而且射击出色，这些特点很快在他狙击手的危险和致命的生活中凸显出来。

先去埃及然后参加加里波利战役的澳纽军团华裔战士的人数不清楚，但可能不多。考虑到严格的身体上的要求以及’血统’问题，年轻的华裔澳大利亚志愿者通常身材矮小，胸围小，常常看上去很虚弱，并且明显是亚洲血统，他们会很难入伍的。比利·辛（Billy Sing）可能很幸运：他只有5英尺5英寸高，体重141磅，仅63公斤。

比利被接纳进第5轻骑兵团，是第二批被派往埃及的部队，在准将格兰维尔·赖里的指挥下。赖里准将也以’公牛’为人所知，他是布尔战的老将，深受士兵的爱戴。轻骑兵团于5月20日到达加里波利，即澳大利阵线遭到约40,000名土耳其人的大规模袭击造成10,000多人伤亡以后的第二天。

比利很快参战。他在查塔姆堡垒岗担任狙击手；他在前线不断换位置，常常与他的观瞄手伊昂·伊德里斯一起，伊德里斯后来成为著名作家。他在昆士兰乡下狩猎并是神枪手的经历使他迅速引起了军官的注意，首先是澳大利亚司令伯德伍德将军，然后是加里波利半岛英军司令伊恩·汉密尔顿将军，最后是战争大臣基奇纳勋爵。

比利每天的惯例简单而致命。前一天夜里擦好枪给枪上好油，他和他的观瞄手会小心翼翼地走向狙击位置，躺在一张铺地防潮布上，开始他们一天的工作。等待，观察，观瞄手会仔细扫描不到200米远的土耳其战壕，寻找任何动静，尤其是散布在土耳其胸墙上那些砖砌的小窥视孔。一旦发现动静，便将该点指给比利等待，比利的眼睛和步枪仔细瞄准敌人的战壕。然后，几乎看不到动静并发出’砰’的一声，比利又开火了，又一名土耳其士兵躺在战壕里死了。

当他于1915年11月从加里波利撤离时，比尔·辛被正式认定为射死201敌人。他的指挥官斯蒂芬·米奇利少校认为应该是将近300。1915年9月8日格兰维尔·赖里准将建议授予比利辛殊功勋章。1916年1月11日官方正式公布时，嘉奖内容如下：

> 因在纽澳军团作为狙击手1915年5月之9月间表现出显赫英勇。他的勇气和技术特别出色，造成敌军中很大数目的伤亡，敢于冒任何危险。

参加加里波利战役的另一纽澳军团华裔战士是塔斯马尼亚州克莱蒙特的纳尔逊·辛，但他似乎不是比利·辛的亲戚。他当时只有18岁，只有5英尺3英寸高，已经结婚，职业是造船。他于1915年6月在朗塞斯顿入伍，进入第26营，并于9月到加里波利参战，在加里波利战役中幸存下来，但在1916年8月的波济耶尔战斗中受伤，被送往英格兰养腿部枪伤。

伤好后尼尔森·辛回到法国，继续与第26营一起作战，参加布勒库尔战役，梅宁路段战役，然后参加帕济耶尔战役、亚眠战役、圣康坦山战役和兴登堡防线。令人悲伤的是，他1918年10月6日在法国村庄蒙布勒安的最后一次澳大利亚战斗中阵亡，当时距澳大利亚帝国军撤离战线仅几个小时，离大战结束仅五个星期。

多亏邱德仁博士、苏菲·库奇曼博士和墨尔本中国博物馆的勤奋研究人员的努力，已经确定了34名澳纽军团华裔战士参加加里波利战役。战斗中有4人被杀，另外8人受伤，其中2人得’肠’热，实际上，即伤寒，一种由卫生条件差、食物不洁或水污染引起的衰弱性疾病。但是防疫接种使死亡率保持较低。发烧持续一到八周。

1915年12月下旬从加里波利最后撤离后，澳大利亚人首先来到了伦诺斯岛上的蒙德罗斯，然后又回到了埃及。在这里，来自加里波利的营被分割成新的营：经验丰富的士兵与来自澳大利亚的新兵混在一起。然后澳大利亚帝国军继续进行严格的训练，从1916年3月开始将部队转移到西线，首先是从亚历山大港乘船到马赛，然后是乘火车奔赴阿尔芒蒂耶尔附近的战场。

第十四章 流血与消耗

澳大利亚人以及包括德国人在内所有军队的人员损失率都很高。盟军总部的态度很简单：谁先损失尽人员，盟军还是德军？人员消耗的问题使英法两国指挥官的思想重新集中在无休止地寻求更多人参加这场屠夫的野餐。

一方对男人的需要不断增长，另一方慷慨地提出提供劳工，谈判进展迅速。1915年3月，第一次讨论失败了，但是战争愈演愈烈且毫无进展，盟军需要动员一切可能的人来参军，这确保了梁士诒的提议很快得到同意。1915年6月，梁第一次主动提供中国人的帮助。法国顾问已独立向驻北京法国大臣亚历山大·康蒂介绍了情况，开始谈判招募中国劳工协助法国的战争努力。

到11月，进一步的讨论已经包括中国的要求，即被招募的任何中国人必须由法国承包商雇用，而不是中国政府提供。康蒂已经可以向巴黎报告说，梁提供了30,000至40,000名工人。法国战争部接受了梁的提议，并在乔治·特普蒂尔中校的带领下向中国派遣了一个代表团，该代表团于1916年1月17日抵达北京，并立即开始进行工作。

中国政府规定了为同盟国雇用中国劳工的三个条件。首先，这些人不能被用来执行战斗任务，必须远离激战中的前线区域。其次，这些人将获得与法国或英国工人相同的权利和条件。第三，中国保留派遣观察员和政府官员以确保尊重劳工的权利和自由的权力。

尽管表面上是'农业'相关事项，但特伦蒂尔使团的工作很快引起了德国驻华大臣欣茨海军上将的注意。欣茨向柏林报告，柏林向中国政府抗议，即使在私人承包商的掩盖下，这一计划也违反了中立性：对盟军的战争努力，一名工人等于一名士兵。中国对

德国的反应是他们的国民有按照合同在欧洲工作的自由，但实际上中国鼓励当地总督和管理人员在本省寻找潜在的新劳工。

在法国的招募过程中很早就出现了问题。在整个战争期间各种争端和事件中这些问题都将继续。1916年10月，法国人试图通过占领天津的一部分来扩大他们的租界，这被称为’老西开事件’。这个事件以及法国人对中国人的其他误解和不尊重使他们的招募计划遭到严重破坏，甚至试图从中国南部招募劳工也失败了。此外，法国的民政和军事管理部门缺乏协调，使情况进一步复杂化，最终严重限制了中国人为法国军队工作的人数。

梁也已与英国接洽。早在1915年6月，梁就主动要提供中国支持，最初伦敦认为这是不切实际的。但是，与法国一样，英国也存在人力短缺的问题。到1917年初，英国已需要在更广的范围内寻找支持。

英国人已经从工业和受保护的职业中找人。在某些情况下，他们用妇女代替了男子。但是更多的人工援助将为前线提供新的人力。特别是在士兵可以从港口、铁路、工厂和工程项目等后方地区解放出来的地方。

英国工会的威胁和抱怨以及开始听到的民众有关种族的担忧都被搁置了一边。英国认为，组织劳力和人力是通往胜利之路，必须不遗余力地将国家集中在重要的战争工作上。

此外，在法国开展的春季和夏季攻势，尤其是1916年7月开始的极其血腥的索姆河战役，使英国意识到除了接受中国的帮助外别无选择。

在英国事情开始迅速进展。在国会，温斯顿·邱吉尔赞成引进中国劳动力，声称会通过为战争做出

贡献来挽救英国人的生命。中国’苦力’被认为是理想的工人：有韧性，廉价，坚韧并且能够忍受北方冬季，这与黑人劳动力不同，后者被认为不适合在寒冷的气候下工作。因此，英国于1916年8月在中国建立了自己的招聘组织，不是最初建议的在香港建立，而是在山东半岛的威海卫建立，就像法国的措施一样，起步也很糟糕。

与法国人不同，英国人没有使用私人承包商，而是使用英国政府的特别中介。最初的招聘很慢。英国人意识到，如果要使招募的人数增加，他们将需要中国当地人的支持。他们与中国政府达成了一项招聘协议。协议包括给英国的赔偿暂停50年，将允许中国政府提高税收，最重要的是，英国将在战争结束时的任何和平协议或会议中支持中国。通过这些手段，英国很快发现自己招到了比法国更多的中国劳工。英国官员领导的劳工单位组织良好，并由军事控制和协调。

对于英法两国来说，保密都极为重要。除了军事保密问题外，两个欧洲国家都不喜欢依靠中国提供援助。在过去100年中残酷无情地对待中国之后，这并不是英国希望体现的好形象。另一方面，中国对保密感到满意：中国不希望日本或德国知道中国参与。中国政府还感到尴尬的是，传统上其公民离开中国会以死亡威胁，但是现在，通过国际外交和对未来的展望，这种情况被完全扭转，甚至被立法通过。希望这些远离家乡的人能够带着西方的技能和专门知识甚至是投资小型生意和创业的资金回到中国。

开往法国的劳工是由一家名义上的私营公司承包的，而中国政府则通过诸如惠民公司之类的前台组织间接控制和监督工人的工资和条件。根据法国的合同，劳工承诺工作五年，为国防而不是军事行动受雇。法国法律将保护他们的权利，允许他们信奉自己的宗教，并提供医疗保健和假期。还考虑到劳工的口

粮（包括每天100克大米）以及适当的衣物、床上用品和炊具。他们身着制服，发了两套蓝色棉服、羊毛长裤、开衫、背心、雨衣、毡帽和金属腕带，上面有他们的名字和编号。

为英国劳工旅选人是另外一回事。英国人使用军事身体检查程序：他们接受20至40岁的男性，但60%的人因为健康状况而遭拒绝，包括眼疾、性病、牙齿不良和其他身体障碍。成功的新聘劳工在获得制服之前须先进行消毒浴、剃光头、剪去辫子。

最后，给了他们的手腕上套上一个盖了印的金属圆盘，上面印有数字和名字。工资办公室就按照此数字付款。还录下他们的指纹，用指纹在合同上签名，防止混乱并创建可靠的身份识别系统。一旦通过身体检查，男子便进入带刺铁丝网的封闭营地（以防止其逃脱），接受包括不带武器的行军和演习在内的训练。

与法国相比，英国的合同不够详尽，对工人的需要不利，故意使人困惑。中国劳工的合同期为三年，而不是五年，每天支付一法郎。每个家庭每月可得到十个银元。英国人与每个劳工单独签约，而不是通过招聘公司签约，这使中国人很难为自己的权利争辩或因为英方违约而寻求补救。尽管只为完成的危险工作提供微薄的报酬，但1918年下半年之前法国和英国的合同都没有为长期伤亡或残障提供退休金或现实的赔偿，即使是被敌方炮击打死或受伤的人也不能提出索偿要求。

中国现在面临的另一个问题是：如何关心和支持这些远离家乡的人。尽管合同包括工作条件，工资水平及其合法权利，但人们认为必须有中国外交人员在场监督和报告劳工的进步和健康状况，才能保证这些权利和条件。这突出了问题。例如，中国劳工抱怨法国人给他们吃马肉。中国人员非常了解工人的困境。

他们在许多场合抱怨并抗议侵犯人权、虐待和合同相关的问题。

出乎意料的是很快就出现竞争，尤其是在中国北部，那里有强壮而高大的劳动力。两国都试图通过建议设立分别的招募区来解决这一问题，但问题一直持续到1918年初停止招募为止。另一个问题是运输的问题，尤其是在美国参战之后。

每个国家都有自己的运输安排，但英国有更多的船只可用。为法国招聘的中国劳工提供英国船只引起了争议：法国人需要依靠英国人进行运送。事情变得如此糟糕，以至于法国人于1918年1月取消了在中国的招聘计划，并在下一个月正式关闭了该项目。在有了来自美国的航运压力的情况下，两个月后的1918年4月，英国也取消了对中国劳工的招募和运输，因为他们知道可以用空出来的船只将10,000名美军运送到前线帮助打战。

1916年年中，中国劳工旅训练完毕准备就绪，有船只运送并且西线迫切需要，第一批去法国的劳工旅离开中国前往法国。到1917年底，’私人’中国惠民公司在约总共40,000人去法国的劳工中已招募、办理、培训和运送了近33,000名劳工，另外有95,000人去了英国，虽然他们的计划是总共招募150,000人为战争服务。由于船运供应有限，一些仍在中国的劳工被取消了合同，送回了家。

看来，约有14万中国劳工最终长途旅途去了法国，但人数可能高达20万。据认为，有200,000至500,000人以类似的身份流向了俄罗斯，但估计数目不尽相同，而且记录早已丢失。无论确切人数多少，这都是盟国雇用的来自任何国家的最大外国劳工队伍。我们可以肯定知道的是，这些中国人为战争做出了巨大贡献，并且在此过程中曾经历精疲力竭、营养不良、暴露、疾病甚至敌人的炮火。

第十五章　屠夫的野餐

到1916年7月，澳大利亚人从埃及的调动已基本完成。这些澳洲军人讨厌炎热、沙子和污秽物。他们很高兴坐在火车上穿越法国郁郁葱葱的绿色乡村向北行驶前往战场，火车经过巴黎时，可以看到远处的埃菲尔铁塔，但是不久之后，就已经可以听到东边传来的远处的枪炮声。

他们的火车旅程在法国北部结束，从那里行军去前线。他们在阿尔芒蒂耶尔周围的所谓’保育区’就位，之所以如此称呼，是因为双方都会派遣无战场经验的新兵到这里在不遭枪击的情况下体验前线生活。但这种做法不适合澳大利亚人的行为方式。他们开始进行战壕突袭，骚扰德国人，但很快就发现德国兵比土耳其兵更狡猾，发现在这片没有沙土和灼热，但充满雨水、泥土和炮火不断的土地上，与他们对战的德国人是聪明、训练有素、好斗的对手。这是一场完全不同的致命的战争。

澳大利亚人的第一次战斗是在1916年7月，发生在弗罗梅勒斯。开战24小时内便有5,533名澳大利亚人伤亡，其中1,917人丧生，相当于布尔战争、朝鲜战争和越南战争中的人员伤亡总数。在澳大利亚第五师的可怕交战中，有9名华人澳纽军团士兵，其中2人战死，1人受伤被俘。仅四天后，于7月23日，便开始了波济耶尔战役的第一次进攻，有32名澳纽军团华人士兵参加这场战役，其中一些会在其中献身。

与此同时，在澳大利亚国内，需要更多男性的压力迫使士兵招募标准和招聘要求降低。年龄和身高的限制也有所降低，许多华裔澳大利亚年轻人发现他们现在够资格参军入伍。对央格鲁英-华人面孔的兴趣也会减少。许多华裔澳洲人应征参军并加入了全国各地以州为基础的营。现在，即使是具有明显中国血统

的男子，如姓唐、尚、卢和龙，也发现自己是可以被接受的。

亚瑟·光达就是一个例子。他来自悉尼一个富裕的商人家庭。他的父亲梅光达是澳大利亚人《伦敦时报》记者乔治·欧内斯特·莫里森的朋友，著名的’北京莫里森’曾向皇帝推荐梅光达做悉尼的中国领事。他的儿子亚瑟在1915年8月入伍时近23岁，单身，身高只有5英尺2英寸，职业是羊毛采购。

亚瑟·光达被分派在第4机枪连。1916年7月下旬战斗开始不久，他就 在波济耶尔战役中受伤。猛烈、集中、连续的炮轰是澳大利亚人在大战中遇到的最激烈的炮轰，他们的队伍伤亡严重。亚瑟·光达在火线上时间不长就被埋在炮弹爆炸碎片然后被挖出来过四次。他被送去英格兰，以便从’炮弹休克症’中恢复。这种疾病的特征是丧失方向知觉、感觉震颤、恐慌和失去战斗能力。这是在重型炮击环境下的时间过长而造成的。

最近的研究发现，不是如最初所想象的那样炮弹休克病症主要是心理疾病，而是脑组织也有损害。亚瑟·光达的病情十分严重，以至医生宣布他的身体状况不适于继续留在军队。他返回澳大利亚，于1917年年中在悉尼退役。

1915年7月，年仅18岁的邮政工罗伊登·唐在巴拉瑞特入伍。他带着一封父亲准许他应征入伍的信，上面写着：’我谨此同意我的儿子罗伊·M·唐加入澳大利亚远征军去国外服役’。大卫·唐签名（东巴拉瑞特维多利亚街146号）。年轻的罗伊在服役期间两次受伤，第一次是1916年11月在波济耶尔东北部的泥泞地区夫雷尔和格德库尔附近，另一次是在1917年10月，当时战斗从梅宁路北部向比利时伊普尔附近的帕斯耶尔转移。除了知道他曾因擅离职守失去38天的薪水外，我们对他的了解仅是他于1919年4月返回澳大利

亚，后来就没有音讯了。

尽管因为需要人现在允许华裔澳大利亚人入伍，但显然并非当时所有征募人都理解或信任这一点。1916年2月，罗伊德·唐的弟弟亚瑟·诺曼·唐也在巴拉瑞特入伍，但最初自己说名字叫罗伯特·亚瑟·贝特森。在他的个人档案中有一张条子，上面写着：’宣誓声明真实姓为唐，名为亚瑟·诺曼’。他在战争中幸存下来，并于1919年9月返回澳大利亚。

一战期间，有9名姓唐（Tong）的人应征参加澳军。他们并非都是来自中国的华人。有两个似乎是英国人。弗兰克·唐记录的出生地是英国的金斯敦，身高5英尺7英寸，肤色白皙，头发浅棕色。他于1915年6月下旬在加里波利与轻骑部队一起战斗中阵亡。另一人是昆士兰州布莱考尔市的汤姆斯·唐，他称自己的出生地为英格兰米德尔塞克斯。他是一名25岁的司机，身高5英尺9英寸，肤色白皙，金发。他在帕斯耶尔村下面的布鲁斯恩德山脊上的激烈战斗中受伤后死亡。尽管他们的姓很明显是中文姓，但是又高又白，两个都不可能具有中国血统。

当时应征的还有两个兄弟，卡勒布·达可布·尚和西德尼·瓦·尚。卡勒布是十三个孩子中的老大，1884年在布里斯班出生。西德尼是老五，于1891年在罗克汉普顿出生。西德尼在因尼斯费尔做工的时候，决定应征入伍。他的华人特征很明显，因此他搬到凯恩斯，因为凯恩斯没人认识他，也许机会会好点。他于1916年1月被接受并分配到第12营，但当他的哥哥也试图在凯恩斯申请入伍时，却遭到拒绝。

卡勒布当时34岁，在巴宾达担任文员。在凯恩斯被拒绝之后，他前往布里斯班，在那里他于1916年6月5日被接纳参加澳大利亚帝国军。澳大利亚应对他的坚持不懈表示感激。他于1916年9月与第47营从澳大利亚启航，并在1917年6月参加梅西内斯的战斗中

表现卓越，澳大利亚官方历史学家查尔斯·比恩在《官方历史》中提到了他，他被授予殊功勋章。

表彰辞说：

> 奖给无数次表现显赫英勇和尽职奉献。
> 在炮火弥漫的战区连续四天
> 他一直担任跑手运送任务
> 将水、食物和弹药运送到第一线。
> 他在白天袭击并消灭了敌人的狙击手。
> 除此之外，他经常主动要求进入敌区
> 执行危险的侦察任务，获得了宝贵情报，
> 并且在非常危险的位置临场创造灯光信号
> 向营总部发送信息方面，表现出非凡的技巧。
> 他的行为是无所畏惧，足智多谋和有主动精神
> 的楷模。

卡勒布在德南库尔再次表现杰出，在这场战斗中澳大利亚人的英勇防守阻止了德军的前进。他被授予在他的勋章上加条（第二个殊功勋章）。他的表彰辞指出：

> 表彰1918年4月5日在德南库尔以及在前面的战斗中表现出显赫英勇和忠诚职责。该士兵的榜样一直是本营的骄傲，但是这次他表现格外杰出，无比的耐受能力，英勇无畏，完全无视危险。在战斗开始前他主动要求去一个很前方的观察点，并在该观察点坚持，直到攻击开始，然后用步枪打死很多敌人，直到他的观察点被弹药炸翻。他在敌火中回来取更多步枪，但被派作跑手，他穿越很激烈的敌人枪炮火，继续不断地运弹药直到连队撤出，并主动要求留在后面用路易斯机枪为撤出打掩护，并成功完成掩护任务。他表现出对危险无所畏惧，是一位勇敢的战士。

卡勒布在维莱布鲁托亚的战斗中再次勇冒战火战斗，为此他被授予军事勋章。他的表彰辞说：

> *他*1918*年*5*月*1*日在*在维莱布鲁托亚表现特别英勇，有主动性，在白天冒着激烈的机枪火和狙击手的射击进行侦察活动，对我们很有价值。他建立了一个观察点，在敌方狙击手不停射击的情况下，他成功传达有关敌军行动的有价值的信息，指引我方炮火轰击敌方阵型，造成敌方很多伤亡。他在没有人接替的情况下维持了该观察点。

1918年8月16日，凯勒布在盟军亚眠战役中受伤，被送往英格兰养伤康复。他一直住在医院里，直到当年12月份乘船回澳大利亚，重返凯恩斯那个城镇，受到人们对凯旋归来的英雄的热烈欢迎。而当年在这个城镇他想应征是被拒绝的。他是一战中授勋最多的澳大利亚士兵之一，也是授勋最多的华裔澳洲士兵。还有证据表明他曾被考虑授予维多利亚十字勋章。

同时，他的弟弟西德尼・瓦·尚于1916年1月上旬入伍，当年于9月加入他的营。他们营参加了澳军袭击波济耶尔附近姆可农场的战斗。在1916-17年的严冬中，他得了战壕脚病，小腿和脚都被冻僵，被送进医院。1917年9月，他曾参加过一门烹饪课程，并留在原来的营中，直到1919年8月返回澳大利亚。

尽管卡勒布・尚几次授勋，但仅次于比利・辛的最著名华裔澳军士兵还是来自维多利亚乡村塔拉维尔的朗蒂普兄弟。1916年1月，六个兄弟前往墨尔本一起应征入伍，但由于大家担心这么多来自一个家庭的人参加战争，最初是三个然后是两个人被送回了家。最终留下的四个人都加入了轻骑兵部队。他们四个分

别是27岁的亨利，22岁的欧内斯特，20岁的莱斯利和19岁的伯迪。他们都加入了第四轻骑兵团，然后被调到骆驼军团。四兄弟全部幸存回来。包括兰蒂普兄弟和比利·辛在内，总共有15个华裔澳洲人加入了骑轻兵部队。

在四兄弟中，莱斯利引起了最多的关注。在贝尔谢，他参加了著名的轻骑部队对贝尔谢巴的冲锋，并于1918年9月30日在向考卡布的前进中被授予殊功勋章。他的表彰辞说：

> ‘该军士为捕获战地炮做出了极有价值的协助，他表现出极大的创造性和勇气。他冒着猛烈的炮火夺下朝我阵地开火的大炮，当一组敌军企图重新夺回大炮时，他占领地形击退了敌军’。

在大马士革郊外发生了一起特别有趣的事情。这位年轻的华裔澳纽军团战士遇到一位英国军官在训斥他的阿拉伯士兵。莱斯利告诉这位英国人他觉得那么对待他的士兵不对，这位英国人不理睬他，他就走上前去，’冲着他的鼻子就给了他一拳’。当时他还真不知道这位英国军官托马斯·爱德华·劳伦斯上校就是那位赫赫大名的’阿拉伯的劳伦斯’。

在整个西线，华人血统的澳纽军团战士都在为战争做出贡献。1916年7月至1916年9月，许多早期入伍的士兵被调往西线参加在法国村庄波济耶尔进行的残酷战斗。战役始于7月23日，在英国人试图攻领该村庄失败后，澳大利亚人进攻波济耶尔。他们迅速击败了德国的守军，占领了敌堡（直布罗陀），然后扇形散开穿过村庄，朝东北高地上的重要风车坊阵地前进。

在进攻早期阶段战死的有第11营的24岁已婚战士查理·尤。他的个人档案说他是在1916年7月22日至

25日间袭击中死亡，毫无疑问是澳大利亚人占领了村庄南部时，德军对村庄展开了强烈的炮击中丧生的。该《营战地日记》写到：

> 在25号大约从早上6.30点到下午6点，我们的阵地遭……敌人猛烈轰击。大部分防御工事被摧毁，波济耶尔一片废墟看上去完全变样。我们的伤亡非常
> 严重，尽管已将阵线减少到最低限度
> 在整个战斗中，我们遭到了来自右方和右后方敌人的步枪射击和不停的大炮轰击’。

在这次行动中，该营失去了7名军官和153名士兵，另有11名军官和358人负伤。’面对激烈的炮火，尽管有许多人员伤亡，官兵们仍然坚定作战’。他们在25/26晚上被第19营换班。到第11营撤回之时，已有529人伤亡，包括160名官兵阵亡。

他们不断推进，澳军终于占领了村庄上面的高地，即被称为风车坊的地方。今天还可以看到一个基石台上写着：

> 位于此处的波济耶尔风车坊遗址是1916年7月到8月间索姆河战役波济耶尔战场的中心。8月4日此地被澳大利亚军队占领，澳军在这个山脊上的伤亡比在战争中任何其他战地上都惨重。

正是在这个地方，另一名华裔澳纽士兵阵亡。他的名字叫乔治・舍克，是一位赛马骑师，出生于穆雷河伊丘卡，在本迪戈入伍。他只有5英尺4½英寸的身高，37岁。按当时的标准来看，他年纪较大。他当时和另一名华裔澳纽军团士兵爱德华・詹姆斯・金在第22营一起服役，他战死在这片血染的山坡上。

该营的档案显示，两人都是从后方调到这里，在波济耶尔附近地区负责运送负伤战友和挖掘战壕。他们于1916年8月4日进入波济耶尔郊区的防线，并立即遭到重型火炮的射击。夜间，德国人对这个被新占领的的风车阵地进行反夺，但遭到痛击，德军在澳大利亚战壕前面留下了200具尸体。

第二天，即8月5日，第22营巩固了自己的阵地，便立即面临德军第二次进攻。这次袭击迫使澳军撤退。澳军发动了反攻，75%的进攻德军被击倒，战地上尸体横陈，澳军重新占领了阵地。这块对盟军非常重要的阵地被守住了。但是，由于激烈的炮火和人员伤亡严重，该营于8月6日撤出，回到战线后面的香肠谷。

在这短暂的时间内，该营遭受了非常严重的损失，参战约900人中有651人伤亡，其中238人丧生。丧生的人中包括乔治・舍克和爱德华・金，他们的尸体丢失在那可怕的血染的山脊上。如今，他们的名字刻在维莱·布勒托纳澳大利亚国家纪念馆的墙壁上，而他们只是在索姆河战场上澳军近11,000名阵亡无坟墓战士中的两位。

另一名华裔澳纽军团士兵也死于波济耶尔的战斗中。他的名字叫沃尔特·关，于1915年8月在珀斯的布莱克波伊营地入伍。他是西内陆地区米卡萨拉的一名矿工，被分配进增援部队派往埃及的第16营。澳大利亚帝国军希望将经验丰富的战士分配到正在组成的新营中，方法是将加里波利营分成两半并组成一个新的部队。沃尔特・关加入了第16营的’女儿’营：第48营。第48营由雷・莱恩中校指挥，被戏称为’圣女贞德营’（也称‘奥尔良姑娘’），据说这由‘made of all Leanes’（’由所有莱恩人组成’）的谐音‘Maid of Orleans’（’奥尔良姑娘’）而来，

因为该营中有许多莱恩家族成员。

沃尔特前往前线，于1916年8月4日越过艾伯特镇以东的塔拉山。从这里他会看到前方令人恐惧的场景，战火燃烧，无尽的爆炸和闪烁的火光。知道前方是可怕的毒气、炮火和死亡的火炉，真是令人恐惧。每一步都在走近这些。在香肠谷呆了几天后，沃尔特继续前进，经过伤亡角，沿着被人称为’亡者之路’的凹陷的路，经过臭名昭著的波济耶尔白垩坑，穿过先锋战壕，进入位于风车坊下面的电车道战壕阵地。

地面开阔且暴露，因此人员和补给品需要在没有掩护的情况下在炮火中运送。在这里，第48营在约900名兵力的营力中将失去600名人员。沃尔特・关就是阵亡者之一。他的遗体后来被找到并埋葬在波济耶尔以北的博蒙阿梅尔附近的塞尔路2号公墓中。这个墓地葬有699名澳大利亚人，其中有370名澳大利亚士兵是不知道名字的，墓碑上刻着’为上帝所知’，这699士兵中除少数外都是在波济耶尔战役的战场上倒下的。

第十六章　远涉重洋

就像许多澳大利亚拓荒者一样，许多中国劳工从未见过船只，遑论公海。但是，他们都为自己能够入选受训并在战争中为盟军做出特殊贡献而感到激动不已。不论往东还是往西出发，他们的旅途都万分艰难、极其困苦且异常凶险。

一部分中国劳工从中国出发，穿越太平洋到达温哥华，在温哥华登上火车，途经6,000公里后抵达东海岸，然后又乘坐另一艘船穿越大西洋，到达英国或法国。而另一部分劳工则向西行进，前往开普敦和大西洋；或者穿过苏伊士运河、地中海，抵达法国南部港口城市（如马赛），然后再从那里乘坐火车一路向北。

从一开始，将中国劳动力运送到欧洲战场就是一项艰巨的任务。德国人曾在卢西塔尼亚号邮轮沉没后暂停实施’无限制潜艇战’策略，又在1917年2月宣布重启，而运输中国劳工的任务随之变得愈加艰难。横跨太平洋的旅行虽然不受潜艇威胁，但大西洋和地中海海域都早已成为德国潜艇舰队的狩猎场。这种情形很快就对中国产生了重大影响。

1917年3月，英国政府请求加拿大政府介入并管理中国劳工在加拿大境内的运输行程。所涉及的劳工数量尚不明确，转运方向为各个东海岸港口。英国政府将支付交通费用，但由加拿大政府管理和担保运输。第一批中国劳工于1917年4月初搭乘俄罗斯女皇号邮轮抵达西海岸。到岸后，他们接受了医疗检查并获得了分发的衣物、食品和被褥，然后乘坐加拿大太平洋铁路公司的火车出发。许多中国劳工在其后大约一年时间中搭乘了多段火车，而这里就是他们火车行程开始的地方。这些劳工不仅在来时乘坐火车前往东海岸，也在战后沿着同样的路线返回中国。

但是，这个计划自有其弊端。若想在加拿大境内通过铁路秘密运送中国劳工，就需要在其离开港口、登上火车、横穿加拿大和在东海岸港口（例如蒙特利尔或哈利法克斯）甚至是美国港口（例如圣约翰港）登船时隐瞒这些人的存在。这些行动需要执行非常严格的安全要求，配备特别警卫队，同时密切关注信件和电报内容并对加拿大媒体进行审查。相关机构也努力阻止美国媒体发布相关新闻，但并没有完全成功。

除了敌方行动和恶劣天气带来的危险外，轮船和铁路运输也难称舒适，并且存在健康隐患。劳工们的容身空间狭窄，只有吊床和椅子用于睡觉，配给的基本口粮包括大米。在一些船只上，安全标准有所降低，救生艇和个人救生衣的数量不足。英国当局事实上鼓励这类安排，理由包括实行战时配给制度、缺乏供应物资和存在战争压力。他们在此忽略了人类安全的要素，也表明其仅仅将中国劳工视作’苦力’。

希望入境加拿大的中国人需要缴纳500加元税款，这在当时是一笔不小的数目。加拿大立法旨在防止中国人入境。建设铁路之后仍然留在当地的中国人处处遭到明显歧视。过境的中国工人也受到恶劣待遇，只有在严格保密和安全的条件下才能保障他们的行程顺利无阻。

加拿大人还担心过境的中国劳工联系已定居加拿大的华人，从事间谍活动。他们将运输车厢上锁，并派遣保安巡逻，以防有人逃跑。中国劳工旅几乎被当成了囚犯。当时有人就这种虐待提出抗议，但似乎没有任何结果。允许劳工伸展手臂和腿部的活动时间非常有限，也没有足够的医疗用品来治疗途中生病或受伤的人员。但是，并非所有加拿大人都抱有敌意。有时，当地的女士互助会为劳工们组织欢迎宴会，并提供水果和小礼物。不过总体而言，中国人遭到忽视和厌恶。

到达法国后，中国劳工被分配到位于法国或英国的营地。不论在何处，他们都会受到军队管制：他们的日常生活、纪律和管理都须按照已批准的军事规定展开。其中包括由军方控制的邮件投递，以及寄信往返中国的审查制度。当局担心本国的军事或战略情报可能会泄露给敌方，也不愿意暴露劳工在前线的待遇和状况。因此也禁止劳工邮寄新闻剪报、明信片或照片，并且规定他们每月只能给家人写两封信。

抵达法国后，中国劳工旅随即在英国军官的领导下组成了各个规模为500人的工作营。这些军官通常是能力平庸、年轻、受伤或残疾的人士。他们几乎不懂中文，甚至提供的翻译也不熟练，而且经验不足。这些人无法恰当地指挥工作，或是无法传达所需的信息，严重妨碍了劳工旅的效率。因此，劳工的工作质量低下、士气低落。当局编写并分发了一本中英文对照的短语手册，但收效甚微。

尽管如此，这些中国人还是很快开始努力工作。许多中国工人被分配到远离前线的法国工厂和政府机构。而那些为英国效力的中国人虽然远离开火前线，但仍身处德国远程大炮的攻击范围之内。

1918年，德国哥达轰炸机的袭击范围深入腹地：他们轰炸了营地、补给站和沿海港口。在1917年9月1日和5日对布洛涅和敦刻尔克的突袭中，有15名劳工死亡，另有21人受伤。 1918年5月18日，空袭杀死了高达60名中国人。此外还有毒气袭击和德国远程炮击对供应区、火车线和中国营地所在地造成的人员伤亡。将劳工旅成员置于危险之中的状况实际上违反了用工合同，也影响了劳工投入工作和保持生产力的能力。

尽管遭到歧视、待遇不佳，中国劳工的辛勤工作和献身精神还是很快引起了盟军的注意。盟军当局为其取得的成就而惊讶不已。这些工人非常勤奋，也在

解决工程问题和取得成果方面展示了聪明才智。很明显，与英国劳工团队或是来自南非、印度、埃及等英联邦国家的劳工相比，中国劳工有能力承担更繁重的工作，并取得了更优秀的成果。在铺设遮泥板方面，这种对比更为明显。当局发现，实际上是有中国工头在组织坦克车间的工作，中国的劳工团队也尤其熟练精通业务。此外，他们每天兢兢业业工作超过十个小时，因此法国和英国当局在所有殖民地劳工中总是优先选择中国劳工。

随着战争的持续，中国劳工旅从事的工作范围进一步拓展。比如道路需要长期维护，尤其是在冬天，而这意味着维护路基和铺设其他路面材料等繁重工作。在沿海地区，中国劳工从轮船和火车上装卸货物，修理运行中的铁轨和信号设备，清洗并维修油箱和卡车，还要维护电力和通讯电缆。

在法国地区，中国劳工在弹药工厂、造纸厂、制酸厂、军械库、仓库以及政府机构和储藏室从事各类工作。最重要的是，他们挖掘了无数英里的战壕，参与了一系列工程建设，例如混凝土炮台、机枪支位和半圆形军事营房等。对于战争最为重要的一点是，他们使盟军士兵从繁重的体力劳动中解放出来。士兵得以充分发挥军事作用，就像黑格将军所说的那样‘背水一战’。

第十七章 - 敌对的结束

在澳大利亚军队中，具有中国血统的人名声很好。据信，在第一次世界大战期间，大约有250名具有中国血统的中国人参加澳大利亚帝国军作战，其中46人战死或因伤或疾病而死亡。

敌对行动虽然结束，但对西方战线上的中国劳工来说一切照旧。战争宣布结束时，他们也许有一天的空闲休息，这可能更多是由于他们的英国军官不在，喝醉了并且脑子不在那儿。中国劳工不会感受到法国或比利时人民的友谊，不会享受街头庆祝活动、女孩的拥抱和亲吻，也不会喝葡萄酒、啤酒或苹果酒。他们会被从这一切中排除，很可能被关起来，被忘却。但是，战争的胜利也是他们的胜利。

现在，中国劳工面临着另一项任务：清理战场，努力使法国和农村恢复到1914年以前的样子。法国和比利时人、英国人和美国人很快就转过来反对中国人。态度改变了，出现的种族歧视达到了前所未有的水平，中国人被指责与他们无关的事故和犯罪。

更糟糕的是，基督教青年会和照顾他们福利和工作条件的英国军官返回了家园。留下的人和劳工之间的摩擦加剧。尽管他们也想回家，但是还有很多事情要做。在潘兴将军拒绝让美军莱作这项工作后，尽管许多美国士兵才在法国呆了几个月，但他们全都返回了家中。因此，几乎没有其他体力劳动者可以从事这项工作。

在英国军事控制下的中国劳工不是在最能满足合同条款的海峡港口工作，而是被派往内地战灾区。在这里，他们被指示收集铁丝网、填战壕、清除危险的武器和弹药并收回尸体。他们未经训练，但发现自己正在处理诡雷、未爆炸的炮弹和爆炸物，所有这些在接下来的几年中都造成了惨重的伤亡。

这些人在英国地区工作到1920年，在法国地区工作到1922年。中国劳工旅是最后一支离开法国的英国部队。在欧洲期间，估计最低死亡人数约为2,000；中国最近的研究表明这一数字为10,000，甚至高达20,000。死亡人数包括约800名在海上丧生的中国人，他们要么在英国注册的船只上工作，要么是德国潜艇袭击的伤亡人员。最大的海上丧生部分是法国客船阿索斯号在地中海马耳他附近沉没，543名中国劳工旅的男子在前往法国的途中丧生。

敌对行动结束后，每个人都从英国人那里获得了服役勋章（共发放了93,357枚），但接着又继续工作。也有一些人由于疏职或行为不检没有得到勋章。也许更重要的是，在授章典礼上，来自中国的英国军官告诉中国劳工：’通过忠实和忠诚的服务，你们秉承了中国的最佳传统，并在东西方之间建立了更紧密的关系’。

然而，对于这些人所遭受的灾难和痛苦或是种族歧视、疏于照管和他们做出的牺牲，都没有表示感谢或表达感激之情。在激动和兴奋的时刻，在胜利的喜悦和欢喜之中，这些人已经被遗忘了。并且一直被遗忘。

然而，约有7,000名男子在法国找到了新的生活。许多人在雷诺汽车厂工作，其他人开了供应中国菜的餐厅。这成为欧洲华裔人口的起源：今天，这些劳工的许多后人仍在法国。法国人远没有英国人那么种族歧视，他们更容易地接受了东方的方式，愿意提供与法国工人类似的权利。

在帮助盟军事业的外国工人中，中国人被认为是最努力、最合作、最有价值的人。最高指挥官福煦将军曾说过：’他们是一流的工人，可以成为优秀的士兵，能够在现代火炮的火力下行为典范’。

然而，尽管做出了所有投入和牺牲，一旦战争结束，对中国人所作的贡献就很少认可。他们证明比其他帝国国家的劳工效率更高和效果更好，但是他们很少获得战争功劳勋章。英国政府甚至试图减少他们的退休金。欧洲人不仅无视他们的战时贡献，还怪罪他们带来了西班牙流感。最近有证据表明，1917年至1920年造成大约5000万人丧生的流感大流行，确实起源于中国，可能是由中国劳工带到欧洲的。欧洲人还因前线后面地区的普遍动荡和骚乱怪罪中国劳工，但这完全是虚假的说法，因为中国劳工中几乎完全没有犯罪记录。

第十八章　回家

战后及在与中国劳工相处的经历之后，欧洲人脑子里占主导的观念是中国人是劣等人。他们在许多情况下都表现出了足智多谋和想象力，但他们的智力与欧洲人的不同等。欧洲人没有考虑到语言和交流方面的问题，包括以下事实：很少有口译员来帮助管理这些非英语国家的人。此外，英国和法国经常委任不适合其他职务的军官来担任管理中国劳工的职位，他们被证明是极不善管理人的人，这就毫不奇怪，但正是这些人的无能却怪罪在中国劳工旅劳工的身上。

英国人尤其如此，他们对中国劳工旅劳工的惩罚常常是残酷且不公正的。他们对中国人的感情和习俗一无所知，缺乏清晰的沟通进一步加剧了误解。他们采用军事法庭，严厉的刑罚，殴打甚至处决的手段。在中国劳工旅上方运作的还有一个混乱的行政机构，中国的招募中心与在法国的费尔法克斯上校管理的英国中国劳工旅总部之间没有任何联系。

惩罚而不是良好的管理被视为控制华人的方式。结果，中国人举行了示威和罢工。他们拒绝接受命令，这导致大规模逮捕，甚至导致警卫开火杀死罢工的人的情况。中国人的自杀事件更加频繁。他们被当作囚犯对待，几乎没有娱乐手段或减轻无聊感的方式，并且不允许他们去附近的村庄或与当地人交往。

法国人对中国工人的待遇要好得多。特别是在战争结束后，他们可以自由离开营地，去咖啡馆和酒吧，甚至可以与当地妓女在一起。由法国人经营的中国劳工旅营地通常在空旷的农村地区，没有用带刺的铁丝网圈起来，也没有警卫。劳工们在居住区里住得很挤，但在工作时间以外几乎没有任何限制。

法国人还提供了司法保护，他们允许中国劳工受

到虐待可以将法国平民和军事人员告到法庭。一些中国人偷偷逃离了英国的劳工单位，重新出现在法国的劳工单位中，两国纪律和工作条件的差异如此之大。法国人也表现出纪律性：也有中国劳工被虐待、殴打甚至被杀的事件。同样，也并非所有英国劳工单位都严酷，也有一些劳工单位在战后中国劳工向英国军官表示称赞和感谢的。

出现的一个文化问题是，如果他们碰巧在欧洲死亡，中国人希望他们的遗体返回中国。这对于英国当局而言自然是困难的，因为当时英国和其帝国的所有死者都被埋葬在法国和比利时他们倒下的地方。但中国人需要遗体返回自己的土地，以便进入天堂，这对他们来说是非常重要的。

为了解决这个问题，英国人为劳工提供了单独的坟墓，外加寿衣、棺材和墓碑。他们在法国的滨海诺埃尔，一个经过风水大师的批准并祝福中国人选择的地点建立了中国人公墓。葬礼上，中国人抬棺，棺材上盖着英国国旗，仪式由英国医务官员监督和报告。

英国以类似的方式确保中国人获得令人满意的医疗。在诺埃尔设立了一家医院，配备了最新的设备和设施，包括X光机和配备完善的手术室，由中国医务人员提供服务。很早就确定中国劳工必须具有与英国士兵相同的护理和医院设施，通常是这样。诺埃尔医院1917年开业时，有1500张病床，16位外国医生以及300名护士和其他医护人员，能够治疗精神病患者，各种眼疾甚至麻风病患者。

当因战争而流离失所的平民返回了自己的家乡、村庄和农场时，他们反对客居当地的中国，惧怕他们，不喜欢他们的衣着、饮食习惯、语言，欧洲人认为他们可能会有暴力行为。对中国劳工旅施加了压力，要求将劳工返回中国，尤其是有病的人。这导致混乱的反应，突然围捕整批中国劳工，将他们遣返至沿海港口，从那里上船去加拿大，然后乘加拿大铁

路，再乘船最后再回到中国，那些劳工们都还穿着肮脏的衣服，处于生病和不卫生的状态。这自然使劳工及最终使他们家庭感到非常难堪。

但是，劳工们回国时带着多年辛劳的积蓄，积蓄用来开办小生意、盖房或改善他们的社会地位。他们还带着对外面世界的看法和理解回来了。一方面，战争留下了深深的伤疤和遭不宽容、虐待和轻蔑的记忆。另一方面，中国劳工团旅成员获得了新的期望和愿景，仅此一项便为已变化的国家的曙光中注入了新的热情、信心和动力。

对中国来说最大的遗憾是他们在1919年1月18日开始的凡尔赛和平会议上遭到的背叛。同盟国完全无视中国的贡献以及成千上万为盟军事业服务的中国人的贡献。

中国派出了由62名官员组成的代表团。但最后，只有两个人在会议桌上有席位，而不同的是他们的敌人日本却有五个席位。1月28日，中国代表顾维钧在大会上力陈正辞，要求将德国在青岛的租借地归还中国，而不是给日本，并撤销殖民租界。

尽管有英国支持日军撤离青岛的承诺，但中国人并没有在盟军方面找到任何朋友，特别是美国总统威尔逊。和约第156条将山东省交给日本控制时，中国人感到震惊和羞辱。他们认为，山东是孔子的出生地，是’中国文明的摇篮’，但无济于事。无奈之下，他们退出会议。

中国国内深切地感受到了这些屈辱，各地都有示威游行，政府收到无数请愿书，要求推翻这条。对中国而言，幸运的是，在1922年华盛顿海军会议上，美国调解了这些棘手的问题，将山东省的主权归还给了中国，日本人被迫退出。1919年7月19日，中国人与来自其他18个国家的代表团一起参加了在伦敦举行的大规模胜利大游行。

第十九章　停战协定和一个新的世界

1918年11月11日的停战协定使澳大利亚帝国军发挥了新的作用。他们的最后的一次战斗是10月6日在蒙布勒安，一战中长期服役的纳尔逊·辛在战斗中阵亡。此后，澳大利亚帝国军被撤至后方的休息区，不再参与战斗。当停战协定宣布战斗停止时，许多人感到惊讶。即使是法国平民的喧闹庆祝活动也不足以说服他们，许多人还在等待英国报纸的到来才相信战争终于结束了。

到战争结束时，据信在澳大利亚帝国军中服役的共有46名澳大利亚华人丧生。尽管华人在参加战争的33万澳大利亚人中只占很小的一部分，但他们绝对全力以赴：有19名华人澳纽军士因勇敢和奉献精神而被授予勋章。

但是现在呢？虽然这些人认为事情很简单，回到英国乘坐第一艘船回澳大利亚，但现实却大不相同。不仅缺乏可供盟军士兵返回其本国（美国，加拿大，印度，南非和新西兰）的船只，而且澳大利亚总理比利·休斯要求为澳大利亚帝国军归途提供舒适的船只，配有通风良好的双层棚，新鲜食品以及一支管弦乐团或铜管乐队在漫长的航行归途中娱乐部队。

当然，这些船只并不是马上就能获得的。因此，澳军士兵先是留在欧洲，以备万一德国决定重新开战，然后他们被慢慢撤回到英格兰索尔兹伯里平原的澳大利亚营地，一个对大多数人来说是非常熟悉的地方。这儿成为了他们的家，他们从这儿出去休假。他们乘坐免费铁路通行证在英国各地旅行，或在莫纳什将军领导下的各种教育培训计划下

学习许多教育或贸易课程。许多人掌握了基本的读写能力，学了诸如汽车机械，羊毛分类和砌砖等手艺。其他人则去了工厂和办公室，有些甚至去了美国，学习专业技能和技术。

在这段时间里，华人澳纽军团士兵没有受到与澳大利亚人士兵任何不同的对待。英格兰的营地沉闷、乏味且令人厌烦，但问题是：’我们什么时候回家？’许多人花时间旅行，与当地的英国女孩交往，很多人与当地女子结成夫妇。据估计发生了6,000场婚姻。这给运输当局带来了额外的负担，因为现在澳大利亚帝国军军士的妻子和子女也必须返回澳大利亚。比利·辛在一次旅行中曾与爱丁堡的餐馆女服务员伊丽莎白·斯图尔特认识并结婚。她当时21岁，比比利年轻10岁，除了1917年6月下旬的婚姻细节外，她没有回澳大利亚，此后再无任何音讯。

像1918年和1919年回国的许多退伍军人一样，比利回到了一个截然不同的澳大利亚。所有人面临的都是缺乏工作前途，没有受教育的机会，人们对他们为国服务及所作的牺牲无动于衷漠然无视。是华人面孔甚至略微亚洲人的面孔都是不会有帮助的，尽管我们对华人澳纽军士所处的情况知之甚少，但我们可以肯定，他们面临的机会和未来的前景会是严酷的。

像比利·辛这样的人，无论获得多少勋章及多么有名，回澳大利亚后发现对他们来说几乎没有什么意义。比利的婚姻是短暂的，他曾在一个短时间内被尊为澳纽军团英雄，但很快就变得悄无声息默默无闻。他回到乡下重操自己所熟悉的工作：在偏远的牧场工作或探查金矿，但从未能富裕起来。他在第二次世界大战期间默默无闻地去世，被葬在布里斯班卢维希切公墓的贫民墓中。

尽管在澳纽军团作战的华裔军士赢得了并肩作战的战友的高度敬意，但在整个社会和澳大利亚华人社区中却并非如此。白澳政策的制定主要是为了防止非白人移民。其中还有恶劣条款，影响了已经在澳大利亚的华裔澳大利亚人们。在社交上，他们几乎不被接受，他们感到不受欢迎，是受排挤的人。现在还立法来反对他们。

最大的歧视来自就业机会。中国工人慢慢得到解雇通知，从联邦政府工作和采矿业中排除出来。许多工作他们都无法获得：邮件投递、交通运输工作或公务员。澳大利亚华人也被排除在商业企业之外。他们无法建立公司或购买土地，也无法入籍。甚至对于那些在澳大利亚已有很久历史的华裔居民或为国服务过的人来说，澳大利亚也不是一个幸福的地方。

第二十章　被遗忘的人们

中国于1917年8月向同盟军一方承诺对德国宣战。这样做是基于一种理解，即中国将在战后和平谈判中占有一席之地。在北京举行了大规模胜利游行庆祝停战协定：6万人上街游行。中国期待在战后世界中占据新的位置。中国人也希望美国总统伍德罗·威尔逊提出的’十四点计划’将成为新的世界秩序和积极解决日本占领问题的基础。

但是，中国陷入了困难的境地。西方列强意识到，迫使日本离开中国的租借地，例如山东省，也会损害自己的租借地。中国软弱无力，对影响或改变贸易优惠几乎无能为力，但日本军事和海军实力不断增强却完全是另一回事。最后，日本人拒绝让步的态度赢得了胜利。当被视作是美国背叛的详细情况到达中国时，发生了广泛的示威游行和对美国的公开谴责。为一个新的民族主义和新的政治方向的兴起敞开了大门：共产主义。

中国不仅从战争中没有脱颖而出得到承认，没有因为她的贡献而得到回报，而且在一件事情上实际上被排除出了历史。

1914年9月，开始创作一幅巨大的圆形全景画，称为’战争万神殿’。 它的周长为402英尺（123米），高为45英尺（14米），是世界上最大的绘画，由多达130位艺术家共同创作，描绘一次大战的一些重大事件，画面上包括了所有同盟国，也包括了中国劳工旅。但是，当美国人参战时，这幅画已几乎完成，在广阔的画布上已没有空间代表和包括他们。因此，决定涂掉中国劳工旅，在上面画上美国人代替他们。这说明太多问题了，这就是我们今天希望记住’被遗忘的人们’的原因。

第二次世界大战的爆发再次看到澳大利亚华人为国家而战。最近的研究表明，在战争过程中，大约有600名具有中国血统的男女加入了第二个澳大利亚帝国军、澳大利亚皇家海军、澳大利亚皇家空军和妇女辅助队。他们也在澳大利亚的商船队、支援队和澳大利亚境内的编队中服役。

如今，为自己的国家而战的华人鲜为人知。这些人撇开了自从他们和他们的家人到达澳大利亚以来遭受的虐待和种族歧视，为澳大利亚而战。

功劳和感谢应属于墨尔本中国博物馆的努力，以及敬业的工作人员和志愿者，如退休荣誉教授邱德宏博士、苏菲·库什曼博士、华人博物馆馆长乔伊斯·艾吉女士和堪培拉澳大利亚战争纪念馆的工作人员。只有这些敬业的志愿人员进行的研究和调查，才使这些将士如中国劳工旅成千上万的劳工一样能被铭记在心。

永志不忘！

后记

阿尔伯特·黄汝宁 澳大利亚员佐勋位

在上文中维尔·戴维斯博士为我们简单描绘了第一次世界大战前和期间中国和欧洲国家的历史背景、环境起因和心态思维。

一百多年来，欧洲大国，特别是英国、法国和德国，利用了中国的弱点。他们试图拓宽贸易领域的影响力，扩大进出口贸易，并在此过程中将西方的方式、技术和民主强加给中国。为了争夺自己在中国的领土，他们制造了中国内部的动乱、革命、民族屈辱，并彻底破坏了传统秩序。

由此中国人离开自己的家园，寻找更好的地方。他们在美国、加拿大和澳大利亚为了更美好的生活而努力，碰运气，当过矿工，提供各种服务和修建铁路。但是他们并不总是受到欢迎，他们难以融入社会，他们的价值观也受到质疑。

第一次世界大战爆发后，需要体力劳动者来代替前线士兵，使用廉价的中国劳工对英国、法国和俄罗斯政府是有利的，就像他们在过去100年中盘剥中国一样。为了满足这一需要，在他们眼中只是'苦力'的这些人，大部分来自中国北方的山东省，那里的劳动力过多，工作机会缺乏。

如戴维斯博士上文所述，向同盟国提供这种默契支持，在政治上也是适合中国的，中国并未直接参与第一次世界大战，当时仍保持着中立。我们读到过关于中国劳工旅和参加澳大利亚帝国军中241名中国血统的澳大利亚人的故事。尽管有种族歧视以及当时的种种挑战，这些人还是与盎格鲁-撒克逊兄弟们并肩作战，全力以赴。

正如我在序言中所述，我希望恢复历史上这一相对未知的章节，以造福澳大利亚年轻人和后代，尤其是华裔年轻人和后代。对中国人的参与和牺牲有了更好的了解，我们就更有机会建立一个更具包容性和凝聚力的社会，一个更好的澳大利亚，在那里中国移民和其他种族的人们可以感到一种归属感，特别是在我们的日历上澳纽军团纪念日和停战纪念日等神圣的日子之时。我个人坚信，了解这一未知而被遗忘的历史章节将更好地促使移民同化，融合，接受澳大利亚价值观和我们的生活方式。

最近，有媒体报道关于在澳大利亚社会中国的影响。我们听说过人们谈论学生间谍。我不知道这是真实的还是想象的。但是，与我们的主要贸易伙伴脱离关系，与该地区在可预见的将来最具影响力的竞争者脱离关系，不符合澳大利亚的长远利益。

请允许我多说几句。中澳之间的友谊纽带可以追溯到几个世纪以前，中国的影响并非新事。2018年，我们庆祝了澳大利亚第一位正式华裔定居者在澳定居200周年：中国木匠麦世英于1818年在悉尼定居。他曾在当时的几个有名望的家庭工作，后来成为一家酒馆的老板。麦先生是众多以澳大利亚为家的华人中的第一个。

据他的曾孙贝瑞·施英所说，麦世英，又名约翰·施英，有四个孩子，全都是儿子。据信他们在悉尼乔治街开了一家殡葬馆。麦世英的一个孙子名叫马丁，就是贝瑞·施英的父亲，出生于1886年，曾在大型汽车经销商哈登与乔斯工作，于1942年去世，当时贝瑞只有10岁。

贝瑞在悉尼城内的马里克维尔长大，在当地上学，十九岁时搬到了其他州。1988年庆祝澳大利亚两百周年有人来问他之前，贝瑞·施英并不知道他有中

国血统。正如他所说，他和他的家人中没有一个人看得出有任何中国人的特征，因此很惊讶地发现他的前辈是华人，事实上，他的曾祖父如今已被公认为是第一位来自中国的移民。

贝瑞·施英有四个孩子，两个儿子和两个女儿。他的孙子尼古拉斯是莫纳什大学一名学习文学和法学双学位的学生，继承了这个姓氏，但正如贝瑞所说，其他姓'施英'的人很可能在悉尼或澳大利亚境内。这是一个令人惊叹的链接，可以追溯200年到殖民地最早的时期，这个过程显示了这个家庭的贡献以及源自一个普通人的历史。

然而，即使在此之前，中国的影响也已经存在了很久，可能早在18世纪。北领地的原住民岩画就描绘了印度尼西亚的马卡森水手为中国贸易收获海参的场景。在澳大利亚海岸附近的岛屿上还发现了清朝铸造的硬币，分别铸造于1736年和1795年。

然而，后来的历史表明这种影响是双向的。20世纪初，在悉尼的华人澳大利亚商人建立了有利可图的批发业务，在这两个国家之间进出口农产品。1900年，富有进取心的年轻商人马应彪（曾是悉尼永生杂货店的创始合伙人）在香港开设了第一家先施百货。1912年，他扩展到广州，并于1917年扩展到上海。他的灵感来自19世纪90年代悉尼的霍登父子百货和大卫·琼斯百货。1907年，菲利普·郭泉和詹姆斯·郭乐两兄弟在香港开设了永安百货公司，1918年他们也扩展到上海。

直到今天，在澳大利亚中国的影响和民间传说仍然鲜为人知，也少人赞赏。19世纪中期的澳大利亚淘金热期间，主要来自广东省的许多中国工人去澳大利亚的金矿区打工，以谋求财富。从这个时候起，俚语'*fair dinkum*'就进入了澳大利亚的通俗语：意思是

某物或某人是真正的，真实的或非虚假的。可以认为，这种澳大利亚通用表达是广东话’真金’’ding kum’的衍生。用普通话，是真金的意思。但是，我们已经知道，澳大利亚与中国的历史联系远非仅仅是与黄金有关。《被遗忘的人们》是我们历史上重要而又不为人知的一章，突显了我们两国之间的纽带。

在凡尔登战役（1916年2月）和索姆河战役（1916年7月至11月）灾难之后，英法寻求中国的援助，要求中国派遣部队到欧洲大陆帮助与德国人作战。中国没有采取行动：它已宣布自己是中立的，直到1917年才正式参加大战。

但是为了协助同盟国进行战争，中国确实派遣了约145,000名被称为中国劳工旅的中国劳工，外加派往俄罗斯的不知多少千的人。劳工旅紧跟前线后面工作，挖战壕，铺设铁路线，治疗伤员，帮助运送弹药。战争结束时，中国劳工旅又留下帮助清理烂摊子：他们埋葬死者，清除铁丝网和未爆炸的炸弹。

英法估计中国劳工旅的伤亡人数为3,000至5,000，但有些估计则认为伤亡人数高达20,000。他们死于疾病、饥饿和战争伤亡。由于他们不是军事人员，大多数人只是被埋葬在倒下的地方。有些被安葬在海滨诺埃尔河畔的大型中国公墓中，或在军事公墓的边缘或边界墙旁。他们的坟墓由英联邦战争坟墓委员会管理。

由于他们的工资很低（他们每天只有一法郎），许多人想在战后留下。但是英国不许，中国劳工旅被迫回国。法国比较慷慨。它允许大约7,000名中国劳工旅男子留下来，这些男子成为今天欧洲华人社区的起源。

在澳大利亚，约有416，809名年轻人应征参战。约有33万人前往海外参战，其中三分之一阵亡或受

伤：60,000人阵亡，166,811人受伤。正是通过这些人，澳大利亚人的兄弟伙伴情谊性格才在战火中而得以锻造。

澳大利亚人很快意识到他们与英国人不同，因为英国人与他们不同。我们澳大利亚人通过坚定的决心、意志和真正的毅力发展了我们的性格。尽管人口少，但在国际体育或商业活动中，国家虽小但战绩卓越，用比喻来说，’我们拳头的力量常常超过自己的体重’。许多有中国血统的澳大利亚人也报名参加，为他们选为自己家园的国家战斗，但大多数人遭拒绝，因为不符合必须具有大量欧洲血统或后裔的要求。

在第二次世界大战中，一些参加过一战的华人澳纽军团老兵重新入伍。他们以非战斗人员身份服役，其中包括尚氏兄弟（Shang）、哈里·霍林（Harry Hoyling）、艾伯特·梁·（Albert Lagoon）、朱利安·平（Julian Ping）、托马斯·谢（Thomas See）、威廉·谢（William See）以及塞缪尔和赫德利·唐威兄弟（Samuel and Hedley Tongway）。华裔澳纽军团士兵的孩子和家庭在第二次世界大战中服役的包括来自南澳大利亚的甘（Gum）家，来自维多利亚的兰蒂普家（Langtips）和列普家（Lepps）以及来自西澳大利亚的善洪家（Shanhuns）。

我要特别提及一些家庭。来自南澳大利亚州的楚克斯（Chucks）一家有五人在第二帝国部队中服役。马卢家（Mahlook）有20名家庭成员，19名男性和1名女性，在武装部队服役。著名中医邝仕德的后人有八个孙子、一个孙女和五个孙女婿都服役。最后，达里尔·洛蔡将军家的五名成员全部在第二澳大利亚帝国军中服役。

第二次世界大战宣战时，许多中国商业海员被困在澳大利亚，无法返回家园。认识到抗日战争和日本

是共同的敌人之后，400多人应征加入第二澳大利亚帝国军的第七就业公司，组成了仅华人的单位。这些人分别驻扎在达尔文、汤斯维尔和布鲁姆。他们担负着至关重要的非战斗角色：他们装载商船，建造小型帆船并为武装部队生产粮食。

澳大利亚人和中国人一直团结在一起。在广岛和长崎原子弹袭击结束第二次世界大战之前，中国是遏制日本在北太平洋发展的主要力量。众所周知，日本潜艇进入了悉尼海港，日本飞机轰炸了达尔文。但是滞留在澳大利亚的中国海员和商人与澳大利亚人和华裔澳大利亚一战老兵并肩作战。

许多人丧生，但中国作为一个国家作出了最大的牺牲。遏制日本侵略中有1400万人丧生。如果不是因为中国努力阻挡日本的推进，今天的澳大利亚会是一个什么样的国家？

今天，对作出的牺牲以及我们两个国家之间结下的友谊纽带，年轻一代知道多少？像任何关系一样，我们的关系有起有落，但是我们有着共同的历史。我们友谊的根源深厚。没有什么关系比涉及牺牲的关系更牢固：双方都付出了很多。为了我们两国的利益，需要讲述和分享《被遗忘的人们》（中国劳工旅和澳大利亚华人澳纽军团将士）的故事。

在我前面的评论中，我提到了媒体报道中国在澳大利亚的影响。考虑到澳大利亚人口中略多于5%的人口是中国人，而且预计还会增长，因此请考虑一下澳大利亚人最近几十年来的发展情况。生姜和辣椒是大多数澳大利亚家庭和餐馆中常见的亚洲佐料。在西方世界没有其他地方可以找到一个国家的广大民众如此擅长使用筷子。随着时间的流逝，中国人在澳大利亚的影响将会增强：两国之间的伙伴情谊将不断增长。

我们的商业利益建立在悠久的友谊和共同利益的坚实基础上。澳大利亚华人对中国也有一定的影响。澳大利亚是并且将继续成为中国的好朋友，澳大利亚同时保持我们与美国的联盟和友谊。在一起，我们都能在一个和平的世界中繁荣昌盛，但这只有在我们不忘记过去的情况下才能实现。我们必须总是提醒自己：’永志不忘’。

想了解澳大利亚的行动如何在其他方面对中国有利，请看桑德拉·皮雷斯的纪录片《1938年达尔弗拉姆事件》。

请点击下面链接了解最大的有关第一次世界大战的画《战争万神殿》。中国劳工旅以及其他人员已被覆盖：

https://www.youtube.com/watch?v=voTiktcgiaE

欲了解进一步信息，请点击：

https://www.theguardian.com/world/2014/aug/14/first-world-war-forgotten-chinese-labour-corps-memorial.

我要衷心感谢维尔·戴维斯博士。是他最初将中国劳工团的困境告诉我的。

我要感谢以下这些机构和个人。你们都在本项努力中支持和鼓励我：新南威尔士州总督大卫·赫尔利将军阁下the Governor of NSW, His Excellency General the Honourable David Hurley AC DSC (Ret'd);、大卫·贡斯基（David Gonski AC）；尼古拉斯·摩尔（Nicholas Moore）；莫里斯·纽曼（Maurice Newman AC）；布兰登·尼尔森医生阁下（the Hon. Dr Brendan Nelson AO）；保罗·蒙克（Paul Monk）；米兰达·迪瓦恩（Miranda Devine）；迈克尔·史密斯（Michael Smith）；彼得·哈克 （Peter Hack）；法国总领事尼古拉·克罗泽（the French Consul-General, Nicolas Crozier）;英国总领事迈克尔·沃德 （the British Consul-General, Michael Ward）；约翰·马伦（John Mullen）；艾伦·乔伊斯（Alan Joyce AC）；杰夫·拉比（Geoff Raby）；思远（Si Yuan）；墨尔本华人博物馆，特别感谢埃德蒙. 邱博士（Dr Edmond Chiu AM），乔伊斯·艾吉（Joyce Agee），苏菲·库奇曼博士（Dr Sophie Couchman），艾米莉·谢亚群（Emily Cheah Ah-Qune ）以及义务人员；安德鲁·福雷斯特（Andrew Forrest AO）；彼特·达顿阁下（the Hon. Peter Dutton）；傅莹女士（Madam Fu Ying）;左叶琴博士（Dr Yeqin Zuo）；埃尔·奈斯米斯（El Naismith）；李柯南（Lee Kernaghan）；诺埃尔·惠特克（Noel Whittaker）；约翰·范·德·维伦（John Van Der Wielen）； 尼克·法尔-琼思（Nick Farr-Jones AM）；彼得·泰瑞（Peter Tyree）；桑德拉·皮瑞丝（Sandra Pires）；艾伦·琼斯（Alan Jones AO）；兰达·范泽拉（Rhondda Vanzella OAM）；玛丽·吉塔德（Marie Gittard）；卡罗琳·塔罗德（Caroline Terode）；乔·奥尔森（Jo Olsen）；希萨·戴维斯（Heather Davies）；沃里克·史密斯阁下（the Hon. Warwick Smith AO）；汤姆·西莫尔（Tom Seymour）；贝瑞·施英（Barry Shying）；杰夫·麦柯穆伦

（Jeff McMullen）; 罗伯·麦克林（Rob Macklin）;大卫·艾略特阁下（the Hon. David Elliott）; 鲍勃·卡尔阁下（the Hon. Bob Carr）; 安东尼·罗伯兹阁下（the Hon. Anthony Roberts）; 纳撒尼尔·史密斯（Nathaniel Smith）; 彼特·安斯提（Peter Anstee）; 马尔科姆·特恩布尔（Malcolm Turnbull） 以及新州州长格拉迪丝·贝雷杰克利安（Premier Gladys Berejiklian）。感谢我们的编辑海伦娜·邦德和本杰明·塔菲，出版人威尔金森出版社的迈克尔·威尔金森和杰西·洛马斯以及广告人麦克斯·马克森。
如有不慎漏谢哪位，敬请原谅。

最后我要感谢我非常怀念的先父黄启阜医生。他总是激励我和我的兄弟无论做什么都要极尽全力。我感谢我的母亲黄邵寄梅，她总是谆谆地鼓励我。我还要感谢我亲爱的妻子苏菲，我的孩子柯特妮和泰勒，他们总是支持我，激励我在这个发现的征途和在分享这个知识的使命中不断进步。

愿上帝保佑澳大利亚和所有生活在这里的人！

参考书目简略

乔·克莱恩等，《华人澳纽军团老兵》。堪培拉：维多利亚退伍军人事务部，华人博物馆和历史教师协会。2015年。

雪莉·菲茨杰拉德，《红带，金剪刀：悉尼华人的故事》。悉尼市：新南威尔士州立图书馆出版。1997年。

彼得·哈克，《上海装饰艺术风格的百货公司》。悉尼：影响出版社。2017年。

约翰·汉密尔顿，《加里波利狙击手：比利・辛的生平》。悉尼：潘・麦克米兰。2009年.

罗，M. ，《1899-1988年，中国移民和华裔澳大利亚人对澳大利亚国防军与战争的贡献》。堪培拉：澳大利亚政府出版局。1989年

罗伯特·马克林，《龙和袋鼠》。悉尼：阿切特澳大利亚。2017年。

马克·奥尼尔，《中国劳工旅》。墨尔本：企鹅。2014年。

潘，H.，《硬币的两面：澳大利亚出生的中国佬的真实生涯》。自我出版。1996年。

徐国琦，《西线战场陌生客：一战中的华工》。麻省剑桥：哈佛大学出版社。2011年。